E-2 Treaty Investor Business Visa Application

ATTORNEY BRIAN D. LERNER

ATTORNEY DRAFTED IMMIGRATION PETITIONS

By

Brian D. Lerner
Attorney at Law

© Copyright 2021 by Immigration Law Offices of Brian D. Lerner, APC
All rights reserved.

All rights Reserved. The petition/application enclosed herein may be altered or reproduced in any way the reader deems fit to meet the special requirements of his or her situation. However, no part of this publication or the information regarding the Law Offices of Brian D. Lerner, APC may be submitted to any Immigration Agency or any other agency of the Government. Attorney Brian D. Lerner does not give authorization to use his name or office in any way when submitting the revised petition or application to the Government.

Disclaimer and Terms of Use:

Effort has been made to ensure that the information in this book is accurate and complete. However, the author and the publisher do not warrant that this particular petition will mirror or be exactly as your situation. There has not been any attorney-client agreement created by the purchase of this petition or application. No legal advice has occurred. The cases, regulations and/or statutes cited may change at any time without notice.

INTRODUCTION

There are a multitude of different immigration petitions and applications. They are complex and full of requirements. Obviously it would be best to hire an immigration attorney to best prepare the petitions and applications. However, this can certainly cost thousands of dollars.

The next best option is to get a sample of the petition written by an experienced immigration attorney. The samples cost a fraction what would be charged by an immigration attorney. However, while the reader has to alter, amend and change the parts of the sample petition to reflect their actual situation, it is a fantastic roadmap for them to use. If the reader has purchased the entire petition or application, they will have real live samples of cover letters, forms, declarations, affidavits and the necessary exhibits to use. The samples come from real cases and the names of those clients have been redacted to protect the privacy of that person or corporation.

These are petitions and applications that have been drafted by an experienced immigration attorney with over 25 years of experience. Get the benefits of that experience without the costs.

About the Law Offices of Brian D. Lerner, A Professional Corporation

Brian D. Lerner has been a licensed attorney since 1992 and started the Law Offices of Brian D. Lerner, APC. The law practice consists of Immigration and Nationality Law and everything involved with and regarding immigration which includes citizenship, investment visas, family and employment visas, removal and deportation hearings, appeals, waivers, adjustment, consulate processing and all types of immigration and citizenship matters. Thousands of families have been reunited and/or permitted to stay in the U.S. and/or return to the U.S. because of the successful work of Immigration Attorney Brian D. Lerner.

This law office handles all types of immigration cases including family based and employment based. Immigration issues range from immigration court proceedings to trying to fix what paralegals may have done that was neither correct nor proper. Foreign nationals must have experienced lawyers admitted to practice law.

This Law Offices of Brian D. Lerner, APC handles cases arising from business visas, work permits, Green Cards, non-immigrant visas, deportation, citizenship, appeals and all areas of immigration. The Law Offices of Brian D. Lerner, APC does EB-5 Investor Visas, H-1B Specialty Occupation, L-1 Intracompany Transferee, E-2 Treaty Investor, E-1 Treaty Trader, O-1 Extraordinary Ability among others. Regarding immigrant visas for the Green Card, the firm does PERM and advanced degree PERM, Family Petitions, and Extraordinary Alien Petitions. In addition to affirmative petitions, the Law Firm represents people in people in deportation and removal hearings, including political asylum, withholding of removal, and convention against torture cases.

Brian D. Lerner has been certified as an expert in Immigration & Nationality Law by the California State Bar, Board of Legal Specialization since 2000 and has been recertified three times. He now passes on his decades of experience by allowing the Reader, Law Schools, Professors and other Immigration Attorneys to purchase sample petitions on every facet of Immigration Law.

Table of Contents

Attorney Drafted Immigration Petitions I

Introduction II

About the Law Offices of Brian D. Lerner, APC III

Table of Contents IV

About E-2 V

SECTION 1 1

Attorney Cover Letter 2

SECTION 2 8

DS-160 Confirmation Sheet 9

Application Fee Receipt 12

G-28 14

SECTION 3 18

Color Photocopy of Bio Data Page of Passport 19

Evidence of Ongoing Residency 22

Resume or Curriculum Vitae 41

Signed Statement of Intent to Depart 47

Articles of Incorporation 49

Statement of Information 51

Incorporator Organizational Action 54

By Laws 60

Source of Funds 96

Holding Escrow Instructions 102

Letter to Escrow Company 111

Lease Agreements 124

Other Investments 139

Monthly Bank Statements 163

SECTION 4 176

Business Plan 177

SECTION 5 212

Declaration of the Applicant 213

About E-2 Application

Are you an entrepreneur? Want to come to the United States to start your own business and/or to buy a business in operation already? Don't have the $1,000,000 required for the EB-5? Well, the E-2 Treaty Investor Visa will require only about $100,000 investment and you can come to the U.S. to pursue your dreams. Assuming you are from a treaty country, this sample E-2 Treaty Investor Visa Petition gives you everything you need to get the best chance of approval. It includes all relevant exhibits, forms, cover letter, business plan and supporting evidence. It has been prepared by an expert Immigration Attorney. Thus, this book will allow you to see a guide of how it is done, prepared and submitted.

SECTION 1

LAW OFFICES OF
BRIAN D. LERNER
A PROFESSIONAL CORPORATION

BRIAN D. LERNER, ESQ.
CERTIFIED SPECIALIST IN IMMIGRATION AND NATIONALITY LAW

WWW.CALIFORNIAIMMIGRATION.US

ADMITTED TO THE UNITED STATES SUPREME COURT
ADMITTED TO THE U.S. COURTS OF APPEALS FOR THE 1ST THROUGH 11TH CIRCUITS

3233 EAST BROADWAY . LONG BEACH, CALIFORNIA 90803 . TELEPHONE (562) 495-0554 . FACSIMILE (562) 608-8672

May 27, 2015

U.S. Consulate General
Level 10, MLC Centre
19-29 Martin Place
Sydney, NSW 2000

  Re: E-2 Treaty Investor Visa
     Petitioner: RK Engineering Works, Inc.
     Applicant/Beneficiary:

Dear Officer:

We respectfully submit the following on behalf of ▮▮▮▮ in support of his application for an E-2 Treaty Investor visa based on his investment in ▮▮▮▮ Works, Inc., a California corporation providing geo-technical and geo-structural engineering services.

Tab Description:

B *Forms*

- DS-160 Confirmation Sheet
- Application Fee Receipt
- G-28, Notice of Representation

C *Applicant Information*

- Color Photocopy of Bio Data Page of Passport
- Evidence of Ongoing Residency in Australia
- Resume or Curriculum Vitae
- Signed Statement of Intent to Depart

D   Ownership
- Articles of Incorporation
- Statement of Information
- Incorporator Organizational Act
- ByLaws
- Stock Issuance/Transfer Ledger and Stock Certificates

E   Investment
- Source of Funds
- Holding Escrow Instructions
- Letter to Escrow Company
- Lease Agreement
- Other Investments

F   Real and Operating
- Monthly Bank Statements

G   Marginality
- Business Plan
- Poverty Guidelines

E-2 TREATY INVESTOR

A nonimmigrant under section 101(a)(15)(E) of the Immigration and Nationality Act (hereinafter "Act"), 8 U.S.C. § 1101(a)(15)(E), is defined as:

> an alien entitled to enter the United States under and in pursuance of the provisions of a treaty of commerce and navigation between the United States and the foreign state of which he is a national, and the spouse and children of any such alien if accompanying or following to join him:
>
> (i) solely to carry on substantial trade, including trade in services or trade in technology, principally between the United States and the foreign state of which he is a national;
>
> (ii) solely to develop and direct the operations of an enterprise in which

he has invested, or of an enterprise in which he is actively in the process of investing, a substantial amount of capital; or

(iii) solely to perform services in a specialty occupation in the United States if the alien is a national of the Commonwealth of Australia and with respect to whom the Secretary of Labor determines and certifies to the Secretary of Homeland Security and the Secretary of State that the intending employer has filed with the Secretary of Labor an attestation under section 212(t)(1).

See also 8 C.F.R. § 214.2(e); 9 FAM § 41.51.

A. ▮▮▮▮ IS A CITIZEN AND NATIONAL OF A TREATY COUNTRY.

The Immigration and Nationality Act (hereinafter "INA" or "Act") requires the existence of a treaty of Friendship, Commerce, and Navigation (hereinafter "FCN") between the United States and another state in order for E visa classification to be accorded to nationals of that state. See INA § 101(a)(15)(E); 9 FAM § 41.51, note 3. As a substitute for a qualifying treaty, legislation has been enacted in certain areas to extend the privilege of the treaty visa status to nationals of certain countries. See 9 FAM § 41.51, note 3.

Australia is a treaty country for the purposes of E-2 classification. See 9 FAM § 41.51, Exhibit 1. ▮▮▮▮ is a citizen and national of Australia. **See Tab C, Color Photocopy of Bio Data Page of Passport.** Therefore, ▮▮▮▮ is a citizen and national of a treaty country.

B. ▮▮▮▮ HAS INVESTED IN RK ENGINEERING WORKS, INC.

An E-2 applicant must have invested or be in the process of investing in a United States enterprise. See 9 FAM § 41.51, note 8. The applicant must demonstrate possession and control of the capital assets, including funds invested. See 9 FAM § 41.51, note 8.1-1. If the applicant has received the funds by legitimate means, e.g., saving, gift, inheritance, contest, etc. and has control and possession over the funds, the proper employment of the funds may constitute an E-2 investment. *Id.* The concept of investment connotes the placing of funds or other capital assets at risk, in the hope of generating a financial return. See 9 FAM § 41.51, note 8.1-2. If the applicant is in the process of investing, the funds or assets must be committed to the enterprise, and the commitment must be real and irrevocable. See 9 FAM § 41.51, note 8.1-3.

1. Possession and Control of Funds

In the present case, the funds invested by ▮▮▮▮ in ▮▮▮▮ Works, Inc. were derived from, among other things, a personal loan, ▮▮▮▮ employment in Australia and personal savings. **See Tab E, Source of Funds.** As such, ▮▮▮▮ has demonstrated possession and control of the funds invested and that those funds were derived from legitimate means.

2. Funds at Risk and Irrevocably Committed

In the present case, ▮▮▮▮ has invested approximately $60,000 into ▮▮▮▮ Works, Inc., $23,000 of which was placed in escrow for the purchase of engineering software, computer hardware and office furniture. **See Tab E, Holding Escrow Instructions and Letter to Escrow Company.** The remaining funds were used to purchase a company car, rent an office space, pay legal fees and purchase other business necessities. **See Tab E, Lease Agreement and Other Investments.**

As such, ▒▒▒▒ has invested a substantial amount into RK Engineering Works, Inc. and he is heavily committed to his company. **See Tab E.** Should the business fail, ▒▒▒▒ would lose a substantial portion, if not all, of his investment. Therefore, ▒▒▒▒ has invested in ▒▒▒▒ Works, Inc.

Furthermore, ▒▒▒▒ is actively in the process of investing in ▒▒▒▒ Works, Inc. The capital infusions are not the last investments that ▒▒▒▒ will make in ▒▒▒▒ Works, Inc. Because ▒▒▒▒ recently established his company, he expects considerable investments in the next few months to a year. However, ▒▒▒▒ is already liable for $850 in rent a month plus general business expenses. **See Tab E, Lease Agreement.** ▒▒▒▒ will also need to invest in additional insurance, labor, materials and supplies. **See Tab G, Business Plan.** In addition, as his business expands and it becomes necessary to hire more staff and spend more on advertising, it will be necessary to make further investments which ▒▒▒▒ is prepared to do. **See Tab G, Business Plan.**

Therefore, ▒▒▒▒ has invested in ▒▒▒▒ Works, Inc.

C.   ▒▒▒▒ WORKS, INC. IS A REAL AND ACTIVE COMMERCIAL ENTERPRISE.

An E-2 enterprise must be a real and active commercial or entrepreneurial undertaking, producing some service or commodity. See 9 FAM § 41.51, note 12. Thus the enterprise must be for profit, and cannot be a paper organization or an idle speculative investment held for potential appreciation in value. *Id.*

▒▒▒▒ Works, Inc. was established in the state of California in 2014. **See Tab D, Articles of Incorporation.** The company subsequently secured an office space and opened a corporate account with JP Morgan Chase Bank, N.A.. **See Tab E, Lease Agreement; Tab F, Monthly Bank Statements.** Since that time, the company has made several purchases/investments in it's own name. **See Tab E, Holding Escrow Instructions and Other Investments.**

Therefore, ▒▒▒▒ Works, Inc. is a real and active commercial enterprise.

D.   ▒▒▒▒ INVESTMENT IN ▒▒▒▒ WORKS, INC. IS SUBSTANTIAL.

The invested capital must also be "substantial." See 9 FAM § 41.51, note 10. The purpose of the substantial investment requirement is to ensure that the investor is unquestionably committed to the success of the business and that the business invested in is not speculative, but rather is or soon will be a successful enterprise. See 9 FAM § 41.51 note 10.1. A substantial amount of capital for E-2 purposes constitutes an amount that is: (1) substantial in a proportional sense, i.e., in relationship to the total cost of either purchasing an established enterprise or creating the type of enterprise under consideration; (2) sufficient to ensure the applicant's financial commitment to the successful operation of the enterprise; and (3) of a magnitude to support the likelihood that the applicant will successfully develop and direct the enterprise. See 9 FAM § 41.51 note 10.2; *Matter of Walsh and Pollard*, 20 I&N Dec. 60, 64-65 (BIA 1988). No dollar figure constitutes a minimum amount of investment to be considered "substantial for E-2 visa purpose. *Id.*

To date, [redacted] has invested approximately $60,000 into [redacted] Works, Inc. **See Tab E.** The amount invested is enough to ensure [redacted] financial co[redacted] because it is a significant portion of his personal wealth. The amount [redacted] stantial enough to make it likely that Mr. [redacted] will continually develop and direct [redacted] Works, Inc. This is so because [redacted] can [redacted] ce the capital that he has [redacted] ermore, [redacted] is completely devoted to [redacted] Works, Inc. and will enthusia[redacted] energy into developing his business. [redacted] bitious but realistic plans for [redacted] Works, Inc. **See Tab G, Business Plan.**

This investment not only allowed [redacted] to establish [redacted] Works, Inc. in California but also enter into a lease agreement for an office space, open [redacted] ount, set aside funds in escrow for engineering software, computer hardware and office furniture and purchase other business necessities, including a company car. **See Tab D; Tab E; Tab F.**

Therefore, [redacted] investment in [redacted] Works, Inc. is substantial.

E.   [redacted] **INVESTMENT IN** [redacted] **WORKS, INC. IS NOT MARGINAL.**

An E-2 enterprise must be more than marginal. See 9 FAM § 41.51, note 11; *Matter of Walsh and Pollard*, 20 I&N at 68 (BIA 1988). A marginal enterprise will return only enough income to provide a living for the applicant and his or her family. *Id.* On the other hand, an enterprise in not marginal if the income derived from the enterprise exceeds what is necessary to support the applicant and his or her family or if the enterprise has the present or future capacity to make a significant economic contribution. *Id.*

[redacted] is expected to draw income from his new business. However, [redacted] also feels that in order to build his new business quickly, profits from the operations should be reinvested in the company in order to build it. Growth is expected to result in more jobs and therefore jobs for citizens and lawful permanent residents of the United States. **See Tab G, Business Plan.** In addition, as a result of a successful career, [redacted] has s[redacted] s to support himself in the coming years. **See Tab G, Poverty Guidelines.** Therefore, [redacted] Works, Inc. will not be the sole source of support for [redacted] in the event that his re[redacted] visa is approved.

Moreover, [redacted] Works, Inc. will make a significant economic contribution to the [redacted] ited [redacted] o the economic health of California. **See Tab G, Business Plan.** [redacted] Works, Inc. will not only provide exceptional geo-technical and geo-structural e[redacted] neering [redacted] also future employment and career opportu[redacted] mmunity. **See Tab G, Business Plan.** Furthermore, as a company in the United States, [redacted] Works, Inc. will purchase advertising, services, supplies and materials from variou[redacted] cluding other companies in the United States. **See Tab G, Business Plan.**

Thus, [redacted] investment in [redacted] Works, Inc. is not marginal.

F.   [redacted] **IS IN A POSITION TO DEVELOP AND DIRECT** [redacted] **WORKS, INC.**

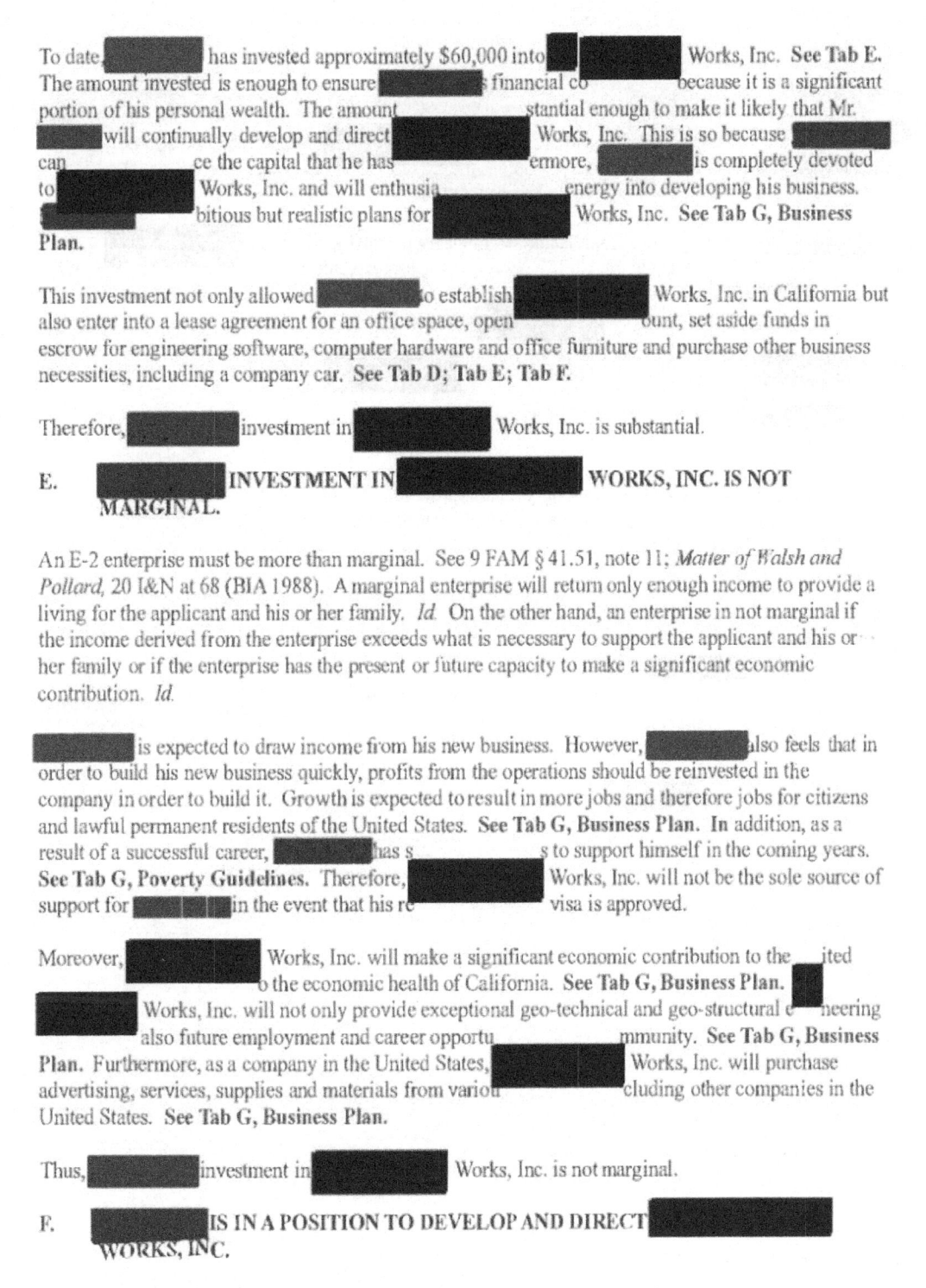

An E-2 applicant must have a controlling interest in the United States enterprise and through ownership or other means, must develop and direct the activities of the enterprise. See 9 FAM § 41.51

note 12.1.

█████ is the sole owner, director and president of █████ Works, Inc. **See Tab D.** As such, █████ holds the top executive position in the █████ has complete control and responsibility for both long-term strategy and day-to-day operations of the entire business.

It is █████ intention to work and maintain a majority ownership interest in █████ Works, Inc. throughout his stay in the United States, continually developing and d█████ pany. In addition, █████ does not have █████ interests inside or outside the United States that would divert his attention away from █████ Works, Inc.

Thus, █████ is in a position to develop and direct █████ Works, Inc.

G. █████ NTENDS TO DEPART THE UNITED STATES UPON TERMINATION OF HIS E-2 STATUS.

An E-2 applicant need not establish his or her intent to proceed to the United States for a specific temporary period of time. See 9 FAM § 41.51, note 15. Nor does an E-2 applicant need to have a residence in a foreign country which the applicant does not intend to abandon. *Id.* Generally, an applicant's expression of an unequivocal intent to return when his or her E-2 status ends is sufficient, in the absence of specific indications of evidence that the applicant's intent is to the contrary. *Id.*

In the present case, █████ intends to depart the United States and return to Australia upon the termination of his E-2 status. **See Tab C, Signed Statement of Intent to Depart.**

CONCLUSION

For the forgoing reasons, █████, through undersigned counsel, respectfully requests that he be granted an E-2 visa for the maximum initial period.

Sincerely,

Brian D. Lerner
Attorney at Law

Section 2

Forms

DS-160 Confirmation Sheet

Confirmation Page	https://ceac.state.gov/GenNIV/general/ESign/Complete_Done.aspx

Online Nonimmigrant Visa Application (DS-160)

Confirmation

AA004VS1CU

This confirms the submission of the Nonimmigrant visa application for:

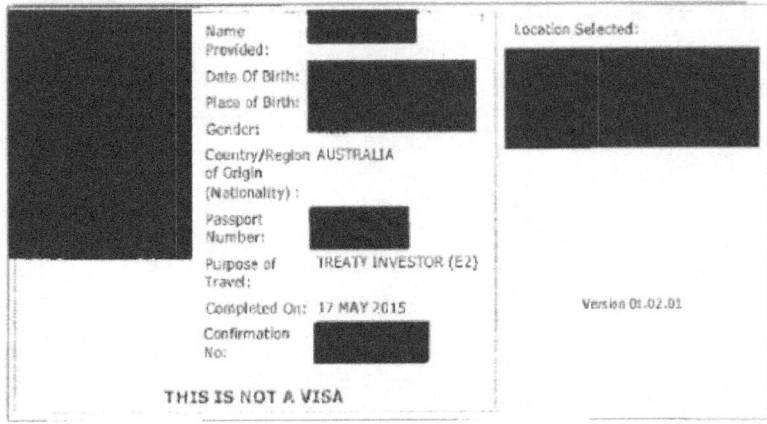

THIS IS NOT A VISA

Note: Electronically submitting your DS-160 online application is the FIRST STEP in the visa application process. The next step is to review the Internet page of the embassy or consulate where you plan to apply for your visa. Most visa applicants will need to schedule a visa interview, though some applicants may qualify for visa renewal. The embassy or consulate information may include specific local instructions about scheduling interviews, submitting your visa application, and other frequently asked questions.

YOU MUST BRING the confirmation page and the following document(s) with you at all steps during the application process:
Passport; Evidence of Status or Investment; Employment Contract

You may also provide any additional documents you feel will support your case.

Instructions

YOU MUST SUBMIT the confirmation page with a clear and legible barcode at the time of your interview. If you do not have access to a printer at this time, select the option to email your confirmation page to an email address. You may print or email your application for your own records. **YOU DO NOT** need to submit the application at the time of the interview.

Please note that you will be required to provide proof that you have paid the visa application fee and any other fees associated with your application. There may be other fees associated with the visa application process. Please check your country's Reciprocity Schedule for any other fees you may owe.

If you have further questions, or to find out how to contact the Consular Post, please go to http://www.ustraveldocs.com or http://travel.state.gov.

Your employer must complete a DS-156E.

NOTE: Unless exempt from an interview, you will be required to sign your application by providing a biometric signature, i.e. your fingerprint before a consular officer. By providing this biometric signature you are certifying under penalty of perjury that you have read and understood the questions in your nonimmigrant visa application and that all statements that appear in your nonimmigrant visa application have been made by you and are true and complete to the best of your knowledge and belief. Furthermore at the time of your interview, you will be required to certify under penalty of perjury that all statements in your application and those made during your interview are true and compete to the best of your knowledge and belief.

You electronically signed your application on 5/17/2015 5:02:27 PM (GMT-05:00). You were required to electronically sign your application yourself, unless otherwise exempt by regulation, even if the application was prepared by someone other than yourself. Your electronic signature certifies that you have read and understood the questions in this application and that your answers are true and correct to the best of your knowledge and belief. The submission of an application containing any false or misleading statements may result in the permanent refusal of a visa or the denial of entry into the United States. All declarations made in this application are unsworn declarations made under penalty of perjury. (28 U.S.C. 1746).

The information that you have provided in your application and other information submitted with your application may be accessible to other government agencies having statutory or other lawful authority to use such information, including for law enforcement and immigration law enforcement purposes. The photograph that you provide with your application may be used for employment verification or other U.S. law purposes.

Application Fee Receipt

APPLY FOR A U.S. VISA in Australia

Home

Logged in as: robilisab2015@gmail.com (2804545)

New Application / Schedule Appointment

Group Scheduling Request

Provide Feedback

Update Profile

Logout

Congratulations! Your payment has been accepted and your receipt is now valid to schedule an appointment.

Your receipt number is 2804545 and it will expire on 5/1/2016.

Continue Scheduling Your Appointment

First Available Appointment is Thursday May 28, 2015.

CGI
©2014 CGI Group, Inc.

G-28

Notice of Entry of Appearance as Attorney In Matters Outside the Geographical Confines of the United States

Department of Homeland Security

DHS Form G-28I
OMB No. 1615-0105
Expires 03/31/2018

Part 1. Information About Attorney

1. USCIS ELIS Account Number (if any):

Name and Address of Attorney

- 2.a. Family Name (Last Name): **Lerner**
- 2.b. Given Name (First Name): **Brian**
- 2.c. Middle Name: **David**
- 3. Name of Law Firm (if applicable): **Law Offices of Brian D. Lerner, APC**
- 4.a. Street Number and Name: **3233 E. Broadway**
- 4.b. Apt. ☐ Ste. ☐ Flr. ☐
- 4.c. City or Town: **Long Beach**
- 4.d. Province: **CA**
- 4.e. Postal Code: **90803**
- 4.f. Country: **USA**
- 5. Telephone Number: **5624950554**
- 6. Fax Number: **5626088672**
- 7. E-Mail Address (if any): **blerner@californiaimmigration.us**
- 8. Mobile Telephone Number (if any):

Part 2. Notice of Appearance as Attorney Admitted to Practice Outside the United States

This appearance relates to immigration matters before (select only one box):

- 1.a. ☐ USCIS
- 1.b. List the form numbers:
- 2.a. ☐ ICE
- 2.b. List the specific matter in which appearance is entered:
- 3.a. ☐ CBP
- 3.b. List the specific matter in which appearance is entered:

I enter my appearance as attorney at the request of:
4. Select only one box:
   ☒ Applicant ☐ Petitioner ☐ Respondent (ICE, CBP)

Information About Applicant, Petitioner, or Respondent

- 5.a. Family Name (Last Name):
- 5.b. Given Name (First Name):
- 5.c. Middle Name:
- 6. Name of Company or Organization (if applicable): **Works, Inc.**
- 7. USCIS ELIS Account Number (if any):
- 8. Alien Registration Number (A-Number) or Receipt Number (if any):
- 9. Telephone Number:
- 10. E-Mail Address (if any):

Form G-28I 03/04/15 N — 4321 — Page 1 of 3

PAGE 15

Part 2. Notice of Appearance as Attorney Admitted to Practice Outside the United States (continued)

Mailing Address

NOTE: Provide the mailing address of the applicant, petitioner, or respondent. If the applicant, petitioner, or respondent has used a safe mailing address on the application or petition being filed with this Form G-28I, provide it in these spaces.

11.a. Street Number and Name: **3 Elizabeth Street**
11.b. Apt. [ ] Ste. [X] Flr. [ ] **4**
11.c. City or Town: **Artarmon**
11.d. Province: **NSW**
11.e. Postal Code: **2064**
11.f. Country: **Australia**

Part 3. Eligibility Information for Attorney

Select all applicable boxes.

1.a. [X] I am licensed and authorized to practice law in the following countries. (If you need additional space, use Part 6.)

Licensing Authority: **Supreme Court of California**

1.b. Bar Number (if applicable): **158536**

1.c. [ ] I am in good standing in a court of general jurisdiction in the following countries where I reside and am engaged in the practice of law. (If you need additional space, use Part 6.)

1.d. I (choose one) [ ] am not [ ] am subject to any order of any court or administrative agency disbarring, suspending, enjoining, restraining, or otherwise restricting me in the practice of law. If you are subject to any orders, explain in the space below. (If you need additional space, use Part 6.)

2. [ ] I am associated with

the attorney of record who previously filed Form G-28I in this case, and my appearance as an attorney is at his or her request.

NOTE: If you select this item, also complete Item Numbers 1.a. - 1.e.

Part 4. Applicant, Petitioner, or Respondent Consent to Representation, Contact Information, and Signature

Consent to Representation and Release of Information

1. I have requested the representation of and consented to being represented by the attorney named in Part 1. of this form. According to the Privacy Act of 1974 and DHS policy, I also consent to the disclosure to the named attorney of any record pertaining to me that appears in any system of records of USCIS, ICE, or CBP.

When you (the applicant, petitioner, requestor, or respondent) are represented, DHS will send notices to both you and your attorney either through mail or electronic delivery.

DHS will also send the Form I-94, Arrival Departure Record, to you unless you select Item Number 2.a. in Part 4. All secure identity documents and Travel Documents will be sent to you (the applicant, petitioner, requestor, or respondent) unless you ask us to send those documents to your attorney of record.

If you do not want to receive original notices or secure identity documents directly, but would rather have such notices and documents sent to your attorney of record, please select all applicable boxes below:

2.a. [ ] I request that DHS send any notice (including Form I-94) on an application, petition, or request that I have filed with DHS to the business address of my attorney of record as listed in this form. I understand that I may change this election at any future date through written notice to DHS.

Part 4. Applicant, Petitioner, or Respondent Consent to Representation, Contact Information, and Signature (continued)

2.b. ☐ I request that DHS send any secure identity document, such as a Permanent Resident Card, Employment Authorization Document, or Travel Document, that I am approved to receive and authorized to possess, to the business address of my attorney of record as listed in this form. I consent to having my secure identity document sent to my attorney of record and understand that I may request, at any future date and through written notice to DHS, that DHS send any secure identity document to me directly.

3.a. Signature of Applicant, Petitioner, or Respondent

3.b. Date of Signature (mm/dd/yyyy) ▶

Part 5. Signature of Attorney

I have read and understand the regulations and conditions contained in 8 CFR 103.2 and 292 governing appearances and representation before the Department of Homeland Security. I declare under penalty of perjury under the laws of the United States that the information I have provided on this form is true and correct.

1.a. Signature of Attorney

1.b. Date of Signature (mm/dd/yyyy) ▶ 04/20/2015

Part 6. Additional Information

Use the space provided below to provide additional information pertaining to Part 3, Item Numbers 1.a. - 1.c.

Section 3

Exhibits

Color Photocopy of Bio
Data Page of Passport

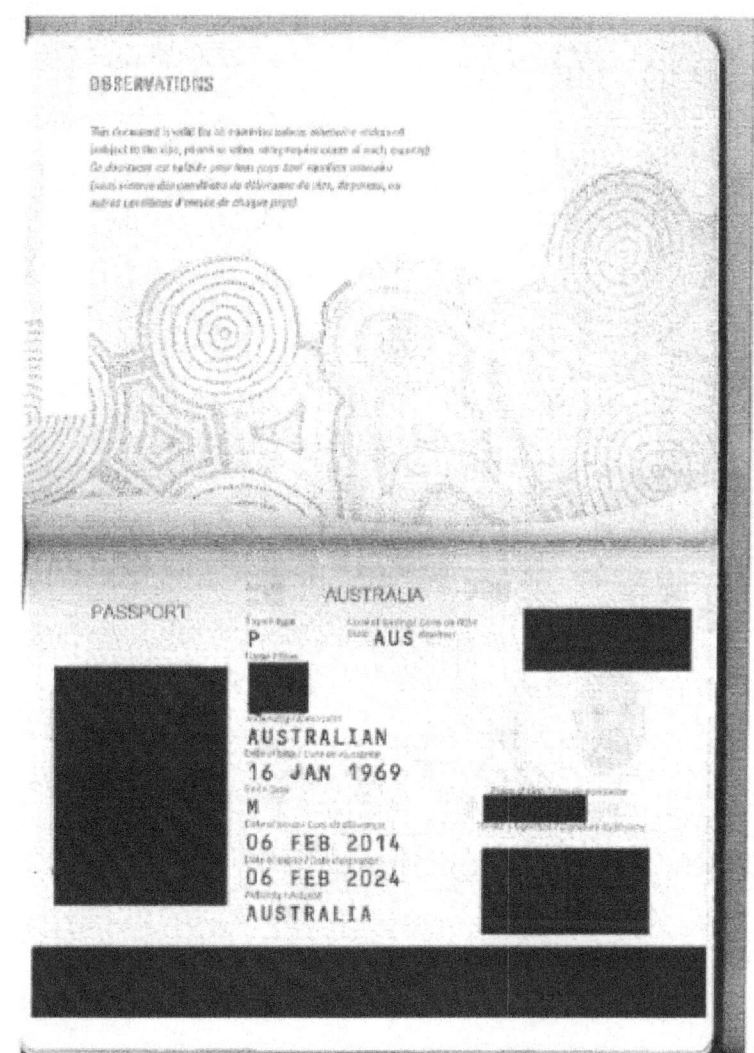

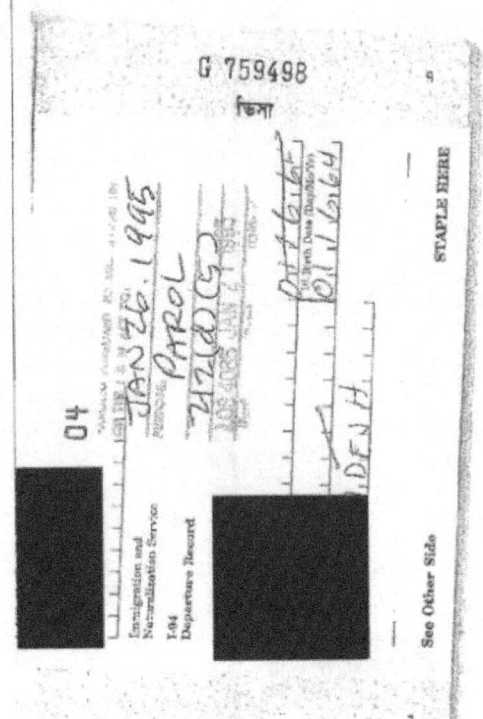

Evidence of Ongoing Residency

TIME SERVICES
Work Centre: PARRAMATTA LEVEL 2
Pay Period: 22/2014
Period Pay Start: 10.04.2015
Period Pay End: 23.04.2015

Prof. Eng   EL3 US10 02
Annual Salary $114,739.00

Personnel Number:

WType	Description	From	To	Unit	Rate	Amount
1499	Period Pay			70.00	62.8276	4,397.93

	This Period	Year To Date	Direct Deposits	
Taxable Income	4,397.93	96,656.88	CBA Wynyard	3,145.93
Less Tax	1,252.00-	27,508.00-		
Plus Untaxed	0.00	0.00		
Less Deductions	0.00	0.00		
Net Pay	3,145.93	69,148.88		

Deductions	This Period	This Year	Leave Entitlements	
			Annual Leave quota	155.76

PSS Company Contribution   417.80
Member Number - 3587767

RITIME SERVICES   ABN:
                                             Personnel Number:
Work Centre: PARRAMATTA LEVEL 2
Pay Period: 23/2014
Period Pay Start: 24.04.2015
Period Pay End: 07.05.2015

Prof. Eng   EL3 US10 02
Annual Salary $114,739.00

WType	Description	From	To	Unit	Rate	Amount
1499	Period Pay			70.00	62.8276	4,397.94

	This Period	Year To Date	Direct Deposits	
Taxable Income	4,397.94	101,054.82	CBA Wynyard	3,145.94
Less Tax	1,252.00-	28,760.00-		
Plus Untaxed	0.00	0.00		
Less Deductions	0.00	0.00		
Net Pay	3,145.94	72,294.82		

Deductions	This Period	This Year	Leave Entitlements	
			Annual Leave quota	161.12

FSS Company Contribution   417.80
Member Number - 3587767

PAGE 24

:TIME SERVICES
ABN:
Personnel Number:

Work Centre: BLACKTOWN LEVEL 4
Pay Period: 24/2014
Period Pay Start: 08.05.2015
Period Pay End: 21.05.2015

Prof. Eng   EL3 US10 02
Annual Salary $114,739.00

WType	Description	From	To	Unit	Rate	Amount
1499	Period Pay			63.00	62.8276	3,958.14
4000	Annual Leave	08.05	08.05	7.00	62.8276	439.79

	This Period	Year To Date	Direct Deposits	
Taxable Income	4,397.93	105,452.75	CBA Wynyard	3,145.93
Less Tax	1,252.00-	30,012.00-		
Plus Untaxed	0.00	0.00		
Less Deductions	0.00	0.00		
Net Pay	3,145.93	75,440.75		

Deductions   This Period   This Year   Leave Entitlements
                                                  Annual Leave quota   159.49

FSS Company Contribution   417.80
Member Number - 3587767

RITIME SERVICES
ABN: ███
Personnel Number: ███

Work Centre: BLACKTOWN LEVEL 4
Pay Period: 25/2014
Period Pay Start: 22.05.2015
Period Pay End: 04.06.2015

Prof. Eng   EL3 US10 02
Annual Salary $114,739.00

WType	Description	From	To	Unit	Rate	Amount
1499	Period Pay				62.8276	0.00
1499	Period Pay			70.00	62.8276	4,397.93

	This Period	Year To Date	Direct Deposits	
Taxable Income	4,397.93	109,850.68	CBA Wynyard	3,145.93
Less Tax	1,252.00-	31,264.00-		
Plus Untaxed	0.00	0.00		
Less Deductions	0.00	0.00		
Net Pay	3,145.93	78,586.68		

Deductions   This Period   This Year   Leave Entitlements
                                                 Annual Leave quota   164.86

FSS Company Contribution   417.80
Member Number - 3587767

CommonwealthBank

Commonwealth Bank of Australia
ABN 48 123 123 124 AFSL and
Australian credit licence 234945

 007

UNIT 4 3 ELIZABETH ST
ARTARMON NSW 2064

Your Statement

Statement 22	(Page 1 of 13)
Account Number	
Statement Period	1 Oct 2014 - 31 Mar 2015
Closing Balance	
Enquiries	13 2221

(24 hours a day, 7 days a week)

Smart Access

Enjoy the convenience and security of withdrawing what you need, when you need it. Plus you can have your monthly account fee waived if you deposit at least $2,000 each calendar month.

Name:

Note: Please check that the entries listed on this statement are correct. For further information on your account including; details of features, fees, any errors or complaints, please contact us on the details above. Proceeds of cheques are not available until cleared.

Date	Transaction	Debit	Credit	Balance
01 Oct	2014 OPENING BALANCE			$1,915.82 CR
01 Oct	SUBWAY PARRAMATTA 0001 PARRAMATTA	5.20		$1,910.62 CR
01 Oct	Transfer from xx0804 NetBank wire		29,251.00	$31,161.62 CR
02 Oct	7-ELEVEN 2173 ARTARMON NS	20.00		$31,141.62 CR
02 Oct	Transfer to xx0804 NetBank	100.00		$31,041.62 CR
02 Oct	Wdl Branch Parramatta	29,130.00		$1,911.62 CR
03 Oct	SUBWAY PARRAMATTA 0001 PARRAMATTA	5.20		$1,906.42 CR
03 Oct	Transfer to xx3403 NetBank	100.00		$1,806.42 CR
03 Oct	ALDI 69 PARRAMATTA AU	7.34		$1,799.08 CR
03 Oct	Transfer to xx3403 NetBank	100.00		$1,699.08 CR
04 Oct	Wdl ATM CBA ATM ARTARMON A NSW 2104	40.00		$1,659.08 CR
04 Oct	Transfer to other Bank NetBank Rent	1,112.00		$547.08 CR
05 Oct	7-ELEVEN 2179 ARTARMON NS	30.11		$516.97 CR
07 Oct	Transfer to xx3403 NetBank	100.00		$416.97 CR
07 Oct	COFFEE HOUSE CAFE PARRAMATTA NSWAU	3.00		$413.97 CR
07 Oct	SUBWAY PARRAMATTA 0001 PARRAMATTA	5.20		$408.77 CR
07 Oct	Salary RMS-PAYROLL WAGE/SA 00985493		3,145.93	$3,554.70 CR
08 Oct	Transfer to xx3403 NetBank	150.00		$3,404.70 CR
09 Oct	RMS ETOLL PH 131865 PARRAMATTA AUS Card xx3398 Value Date: 06/10/2014	10.00		$3,394.70 CR
09 Oct	Transfer to xx3403 NetBank	20.00		$3,374.70 CR
09 Oct	PIZZA HUT EXPRESS LANE COVE AU	9.90		$3,364.80 CR

PAGE 27

Statement 22 (Page 2 of 13)

Account Number

Date	Transaction	Debit	Credit	Balance
09 Oct	BLOCKBUSTER LANECOVE LANE COVE NSW AU	28.00		$3,336.80 CR
10 Oct	Wdl ATM CBA ATM PARRAMATTA B NSW 2223	20.00		$3,316.80 CR
11 Oct	Direct Credit 015884 AUS GOV FAMLIES FB1K3798281 230356L		46.96	$3,363.76 CR
11 Oct	RMS ETOLL PH 131865 PARRAMATTA AUS Card xx2398 Value Date: 08/10/2014	10.00		$3,353.76 CR
12 Oct	HOYTS CORPORATION CHATSWOOD NSW 04	40.00		$3,313.76 CR
12 Oct	COLES CHATSWOOD NSW AU	33.28		$3,280.48 CR
13 Oct	Transfer to xx3403 NetBank	30.00		$3,250.48 CR
13 Oct	7-ELEVEN 2085 PARRAMATTA NS	40.00		$3,210.48 CR
14 Oct	Transfer to xx3403 NetBank	45.00		$3,165.48 CR
15 Oct	Transfer to xx3403 NetBank	100.00		$3,065.48 CR
15 Oct	GUZMAN Y GOMEZ WESTF PARRAMATTA NSW	11.90		$3,053.58 CR
15 Oct	TARGET PARRAMATTA NSW AU	35.00		$3,018.58 CR
15 Oct	COTTON ON KIDS PARRAMATTA NS	19.95		$2,998.63 CR
16 Oct	SUBWAY PARRAMATTA 0001 PARRAMATTA	5.20		$2,993.43 CR
17 Oct	TELSTRA CORP LTD NetBank BPAY 23796 2006149885210	55.00		$2,938.43 CR
17 Oct	MCDONALDS WYNYARD RA0493 SYDNEY	10.30		$2,928.13 CR
18 Oct	Transfer to xx3403 NetBank	60.00		$2,868.13 CR
18 Oct	Transfer to xx3403 NetBank	40.00		$2,828.13 CR
18 Oct	Transfer to other Bank NetBank Rent	1,112.00		$1,716.13 CR
18 Oct	Wdl ATM CBA ATM LINDFIELD NSW 2195	60.00		$1,656.13 CR
18 Oct	LINDFIELD PHARMACY 0001 LINDFIELD	9.50		$1,646.63 CR
18 Oct	ALDI 73 CHATSWOOD AU	91.46		$1,555.17 CR
18 Oct	RED DOLLAR PTY LTD CHATSWOOD NSW	17.00		$1,538.17 CR
18 Oct	TOYS'R'US 4915 CHATSWOOD REG 6 NSW	26.91		$1,511.26 CR
19 Oct	ALDI 73 CHATSWOOD AU	37.92		$1,473.34 CR
19 Oct	ALDI 73 CHATSWOOD AU	16.40		$1,456.94 CR
19 Oct	Transfer to xx5967 NetBank	1,350.00		$106.94 CR
20 Oct	7-ELEVEN 2085 PARRAMATTA NS	20.00		$86.94 CR
21 Oct	Transfer from xx5967 NetBank		100.00	$186.94 CR
21 Oct	COFFEE HOUSE CAFE PARRAMATTA NSW AU	9.30		$177.64 CR
21 Oct	Wdl ATM CBA ATM PARRAMATTA D NSW 2223	20.00		$157.64 CR
21 Oct	Transfer to xx3403 NetBank	80.00		$77.64 CR
21 Oct	Salary RMS-PAYROLL WAGE/SA 00965493		3,145.93	$3,223.57 CR

Statement 22 (Page 3 of 13)

Account Number

Date	Transaction	Debit	Credit	Balance
22 Oct	NANDOS PARRAMATTA AU	29.25		$3,194.32 CR
22 Oct	NANDOS PARRAMATTA AU	10.40		$3,183.92 CR
22 Oct	Transfer to xx3403 NetBank	200.00		$2,983.92 CR
23 Oct	7-ELEVEN 2173 ARTARMON NS	20.00		$2,963.92 CR
23 Oct	MAY'S MART PL ARTARMON NSW	42.80		$2,921.12 CR
24 Oct	ALLIANZ INSURE C1 SYDNEY NS AUS Card xx3398 Value Date: 22/10/2014	99.88		$2,821.24 CR
24 Oct	Transfer to xx3403 NetBank	40.00		$2,781.24 CR
24 Oct	ALDI 69 PARRAMATTA AU	14.91		$2,766.33 CR
25 Oct	Direct Credit 015884 AUS GOV FAMILIES FB1K4168281230356L		46.96	$2,813.29 CR
25 Oct	MADUNIT PTY LTD CHATSWOOD NSW	12.80		$2,800.49 CR
25 Oct	CHEMIST WAREHOUSE CHATSWOOD	9.99		$2,790.50 CR
25 Oct	DAISO CHATSWOOD NS	33.60		$2,756.90 CR
25 Oct	ALDI 73 CHATSWOOD AU	21.44		$2,735.46 CR
25 Oct	KMART CHATSWOOD NSW AU	103.50		$2,631.96 CR
27 Oct	EnergyAustralia Pty NetBank BPAY 97410 10029776998426	56.24		$2,575.72 CR
27 Oct	OPTUS BILLING NetBank BPAY 3061 90119477000183	100.00		$2,475.72 CR
27 Oct	OPTUS BILLING NetBank BPAY 3061 90119477000183	84.81		$2,390.91 CR
27 Oct	GUZMAN Y GOMEZ WESTF PARRAMATTA NSW	11.90		$2,379.01 CR
27 Oct	Transfer to xx3403 NetBank	40.00		$2,339.01 CR
27 Oct	Wdl ATM CBA ATM ARTARMON B NSW 2104	40.00		$2,299.01 CR
28 Oct	7-ELEVEN 2173 ARTARMON NS	40.00		$2,259.01 CR
28 Oct	Transfer to xx3403 NetBank	100.00		$2,159.01 CR
28 Oct	SUBWAY PARRAMATTA 0001 PARRAMATTA	5.00		$2,154.01 CR
29 Oct	Transfer to xx3403 NetBank	40.00		$2,114.01 CR
30 Oct	Transfer to xx3403 NetBank	60.00		$2,054.01 CR
30 Oct	Transfer to xx3403 NetBank	25.00		$2,029.01 CR
30 Oct	Transfer to xx3403 NetBank	15.00		$2,014.01 CR
31 Oct	Transfer to xx3403 NetBank	60.00		$1,954.01 CR
31 Oct	PIZZA HUT EXPRESS LANE COVE AU	14.85		$1,939.16 CR
31 Oct	WOOLWORTHS 1103 LANE COVE NSW AU	16.13		$1,923.03 CR
31 Oct	WOOLWORTHS 1103 LANE COVE NSW AU	4.50		$1,918.53 CR
01 Nov	Transfer to other Bank NetBank Rent	1,112.00		$806.53 CR
03 Nov	Transfer to xx3403 NetBank	40.00		$766.53 CR
04 Nov	Transfer to xx3403 NetBank	50.00		$716.53 CR
04 Nov	Salary RMS-PAYROLL WAGE/SA 00965493		3,145.95	$3,862.48 CR
04 Nov	Transfer to xx3403 NetBank	20.00		$3,842.48 CR
05 Nov	7-ELEVEN 2173 ARTARMON NS	20.00		$3,822.48 CR
05 Nov	Transfer to xx3403 NetBank	30.00		$3,792.48 CR
06 Nov	Transfer to xx3403 NetBank	100.00		$3,692.48 CR

Statement 22 (Page 4 of 13)

Account Number

Date	Transaction	Debit	Credit	Balance
06 Nov	Wdl ATM CBA ATM WF PARRAMATTA6 NSW 2443	20.00		$3,672.48 CR
06 Nov	ALDI 69 PARRAMATTA AU	17.56		$3,654.92 CR
06 Nov	JB HI FI PARRAMATTA NS	7.95		$3,646.97 CR
07 Nov	GREATER UNION TOP RYDE NSW 03	79.00		$3,567.97 CR
08 Nov	Direct Credit 015884 AUS GOV FAMILIES FB1K4578281230356L		46.96	$3,614.93 CR
08 Nov	Transfer to xx3403 NetBank	100.00		$3,514.93 CR
09 Nov	Wdl ATM CBA ATM WF CHATSWOOD 1 NSW 2140	20.00		$3,494.93 CR
09 Nov	FRUTESH CHATSWOOD NSW2	10.15		$3,484.78 CR
09 Nov	ALDI 73 CHATSWOOD AU	56.93		$3,427.85 CR
10 Nov	7-ELEVEN 2085 PARRAMATTA NS	30.00		$3,397.85 CR
11 Nov	Transfer to xx3403 NetBank	30.00		$3,367.85 CR
12 Nov	Transfer to xx3403 NetBank	30.00		$3,337.85 CR
12 Nov	ORIGIN ENERGY NetBank BPAY 130112 200000276523	249.20		$3,088.65 CR
13 Nov	PARRAMATTA VI Cash-Out $10.00 Purchase $8.35	18.35		$3,070.30 CR
14 Nov	Transfer to xx3403 NetBank	100.00		$2,970.30 CR
14 Nov	Trans fer to xx3403NetBank	20.00		$2,950.30 CR
14 Nov	KMART CHATSWOOD NSW AU	70.00		$2,880.30 CR
15 Nov	7-ELEVEN 2179 ARTARMON NS	16.01		$2,864.29 CR
15 Nov	ACE MECHANICAL RPR TOP RYDE	37.40		$2,826.89 CR
15 Nov	ZARA AUSTRALIA 7089 NORTH RYDE	59.90		$2,766.99 CR
15 Nov	Transfer to other Bank NetBank Rent	1,112.00		$1,654.99 CR
17 Nov	EnergyAustrali aPty NetBank BPAY 97410 10029776998426	100.00		$1,554.99 CR
17 Nov	Transfer to xx3403 NetBank	20.00		$1,534.99 CR
17 Nov	Trans feto xx3403 NetBank	10.00		$1,524.99 CR
18 Nov	Transfer to xx3403 NetBank	100.00		$1,424.99 CR
18 Nov	Salary RMS-PAYROLL WAGE/SA 00966493		3,145.93	$4,570.92 CR
19 Nov	Transfer to xx0219 NetBank Green slip	400.00		$4,170.92 CR
19 Nov	Transfer to xx3403 NetBank	40.00		$4,130.92 CR
19 Nov	Transfer to xx5967 NetBank Loan pmt	3,000.00		$1,130.92 CR
19 Nov	Transfer to xx0219 NetBank Pmt	170.00		$960.92 CR
20 Nov	Trans fer to xx3403 NetBank	40.00		$920.92 CR
20 Nov	Transfer to xx3403 NetBank	20.00		$900.92 CR
22 Nov	SUBWAY ARTARMON ARTARMON NS	15.40		$885.52 CR
22 Nov	7-ELEVEN 2173 ARTARMON NS	9.49		$876.03 CR
23 Nov	ALDI EASTLAKES AU	101.54		$774.49 CR
24 Nov	Wdl ATM CBA ATM CBA TOWER 2 NSW 2223	20.00		$754.49 CR
25 Nov	Transfer to xx3403 NetBank	40.00		$714.49 CR
25 Nov	7-ELEVEN 2085 PARRAMATTA NS	20.00		$694.49 CR

Statement 22 (Page 5 of 13)

Account Number

Date	Transaction	Debit	Credit	Balance
26 Nov	ALLIANZ INSURE C1 SYDNEY NS AUS Card xx3398 Value Date: 24/11/2014	99.88		$594.61 CR
26 Nov	Transfer to xx3403 NetBank	30.00		$564.61 CR
26 Nov	Wdl ATM CBA ATM PARRAMATTA B NSW 2223	20.00		$544.61 CR
26 Nov	OPTUS BILLING NetBank BPAY 3061 90119477000183	100.00		$444.61 CR
27 Nov	Transfer to xx3403 NetBank	20.00		$424.61 CR
27 Nov	ESPRESSO BAR 101 PARRAMATTA NSW	11.70		$412.91 CR
27 Nov	7-ELEVEN 2085 PARRAMATTA NS	10.00		$402.91 CR
28 Nov	Transfer to xx3403 NetBank	90.00		$312.91 CR
28 Nov	Transfer to xx3403 NetBank	30.00		$282.91 CR
01 Dec	Credit Interest		0.05	$282.96 CR
01 Dec	OPTUS BILLING NetBank BPAY 3061 90119477000183	60.00		$222.96 CR
01 Dec	Transfer to xx3403 NetBank	25.00		$197.96 CR
02 Dec	Transfer to xx3403 NetBank	45.00		$152.96 CR
02 Dec	Salary RMS-PAYROLL WAGE/SA 00965493		3,145.93	$3,298.89 CR
03 Dec	Transfer to xx3403 NetBank	20.00		$3,278.89 CR
04 Dec	RMS ETOLL PH 131865 PARRAMATTA AUS Card xx3398 Value Date: 01/12/2014	10.00		$3,268.89 CR
04 Dec	7-ELEVEN 2173 ARTARMON NS	20.00		$3,248.89 CR
04 Dec	Transfer to xx3403 NetBank	150.00		$3,098.89 CR
04 Dec	ALDI 69 PARRAMATTA AU	27.29		$3,071.60 CR
05 Dec	VODAFONE POSTPAID NetBank BPAY 52225 841942965	41.28		$3,030.32 CR
05 Dec	Wdl ATM CBA ATM PARRAMATTA C NSW 2223	20.00		$3,010.32 CR
06 Dec	ALDI EASTLAKES AU	37.22		$2,973.10 CR
06 Dec	BROTHERS MEAT GROCERY EASTLAKES NSWAU	124.90		$2,848.20 CR
06 Dec	BROTHERS MEAT GROCERY EASTLAKES NSWAU	8.00		$2,840.20 CR
07 Dec	MAD MEX MACQUARIE SH NORTH RYDE NSW	52.00		$2,788.20 CR
07 Dec	Transfer to xx3403 NetBank	50.00		$2,738.20 CR
07 Dec	H&M HENNES AND MAURI MACQUARIE PARNS	79.80		$2,658.40 CR
07 Dec	H&M HENNES AND MAURI MACQUARIE PARNS	60.70		$2,597.70 CR
07 Dec	COLETTE BY COLETTE H NORTH RYDE NS	29.24		$2,568.46 CR
07 Dec	TARGET MACQUARIE NSW AU	11.05		$2,557.41 CR
07 Dec	SUBWAY ARTARMON ARTARMON NS	8.45		$2,548.96 CR
08 Dec	EnergyAustralia Pty NetBank BPAY 97410 10029776998426	200.00		$2,348.96 CR
08 Dec	ALDI 69 PARRAMATTA AU	27.76		$2,321.20 CR
09 Dec	Transfer to xx3403 NetBank	20.00		$2,301.20 CR
10 Dec	Transfer to xx3403 NetBank	100.00		$2,201.20 CR
10 Dec	7-ELEVEN 2173 ARTARMON NS	20.00		$2,181.20 CR
10 Dec	Transfer to xx3403 NetBank	120.00		$2,061.20 CR
12 Dec	TELSTRA CORP LTD NetBank BPAY 23796 2000149685210	45.00		$2,016.20 CR

Statement 22 (Page 6 of 13)

Account Number

Date Transaction	Debit	Credit	Balance
13 Dec Transfer to other Bank NetBank Rent	1,112.00		$904.20 CR
13 Dec Wdl ATM CBA ATM ARTARMON A NSW 2104	80.00		$824.20 CR
13 Dec ALDI 73 CHATSWOOD AU	66.23		$757.97 CR
14 Dec EVERGREEN FRUIT MARK ARTARMON NSW	16.78		$741.19 CR
15 Dec Transfer to xx3403 NetBank	40.00		$701.19 CR
16 Dec Transfer to xx3403 NetBank	30.00		$671.19 CR
16 Dec 7-ELEVEN 2179 ARTARMON NS	20.05		$651.14 CR
16 Dec EnergyAustralia Pty NetBank BPAY 97410 10029776998426	61.00		$590.14 CR
16 Dec Salary RMS-PAYROLL WAGE/SA 00965493		3,145.93	$3,736.07 CR
18 Dec Transfer to xx3403 NetBank	150.00		$3,586.07 CR
18 Dec BLOCKBUSTER LANECOVE LANE COVE NSWAU	70.90		$3,515.17 CR
19 Dec 7-ELEVEN 2179 ARTARMON NS	20.93		$3,494.24 CR
19 Dec Transfer to xx3893 NetBank	3,000.00		$494.24 CR
19 Dec GUZMAN Y GOMEZ WESTF PARRAMATTA NSW	8.50		$485.74 CR
19 Dec DAISO PARRAMATTA NS	8.40		$477.34 CR
19 Dec Transfer from xx3893 NetBank shopping		800.00	$1,277.34 CR
19 Dec Transfer to xx0219 NetBank Ps4	489.00		$788.34 CR
19 Dec HOYTS CORPORATION CHATSWOOD NSW 02	54.90		$733.44 CR
20 Dec KMART CHATSWOOD NSW AU	28.00		$705.44 CR
20 Dec HANDYWAY GUMBOOTS C 0001 CHATSWOOD	31.90		$673.54 CR
20 Dec Wdl ATM CBA ATM CHATSWOOD CH 2 NSW 2844	20.00		$653.54 CR
20 Dec HANDYWAY EB GAMES 1236 CHATSWOOD	12.00		$641.54 CR
20 Dec FOOD CHASE PTY LTD CHATSWOOD NSW	0.68		$640.86 CR
20 Dec FOOD CHASE PTY LTD CHATSWOOD NSW	20.00		$620.86 CR
21 Dec CHEMIST WAREHOUSE CHATSWOOD AU	32.79		$588.07 CR
21 Dec KMART CHATSWOOD NSW AU	119.00		$469.07 CR
21 Dec 7-ELEVEN 2179 ARTARMON NS	25.08		$443.99 CR
21 Dec IKEA TEMPE AU	216.85		$227.14 CR
21 Dec BROTHERS MEAT GROCERY EASTLAKES NSWAU	109.50		$117.64 CR
22 Dec Transfer from xx3893 NetBank Shopping		600.00	$717.64 CR
22 Dec SES PARRAMATTA PARRAMATTA AU	55.98		$661.66 CR
22 Dec Transfer to xx3403 NetBank	500.00		$161.66 CR
24 Dec ALLIANZ INSURE C1 SYDNEY NS AUS Card xx3398 Value Date: 22/12/2014	99.88		$61.78 CR
25 Dec RMS ETOLL PH 131865 PARRAMATTA AUS Card xx3398 Value Date: 22/12/2014	10.00		$51.78 CR
26 Dec Wdl ATM CBA ATM MACQUARIE S/C2 NSW 2320	20.00		$31.78 CR
27 Dec Transfer from xx5967 NetBank		300.00	$331.78 CR
29 Dec Wdl ATM CBA ATM EASTLAKES S/C NSW 2239	20.00		$311.78 CR
30 Dec Transfer to xx3403 NetBank	40.00		$271.78 CR

PAGE 32

Statement 22 (Page 7 of 13)

Account Number

Date	Transaction	Debit	Credit	Balance
30 Dec	EnergyAustralia Pty NetBank BPAY 97410 10029776998426	61.77		$210.01 CR
30 Dec	Salary RMS-PAYROLL WAGE/SA 00965493		3,145.92	$3,355.93 CR
31 Dec	ALDI 73 CHATSWOOD NS AUS Card xx1281 Value Date: 28/12/2014	50.26		$3,305.67 CR
31 Dec	Transfer to xx3403 NetBank	50.00		$3,255.67 CR
31 Dec	Wdl ATM CBA ATM ARTARMON A NSW 2104	20.00		$3,235.67 CR
31 Dec	Wdl ATM CBA ATM ARTARMON A NSW 2104	20.00		$3,215.67 CR
31 Dec	Wdl ATM CBA ATM TOWN HALL D NSW 2028	100.00		$3,115.67 CR
01 Jan	RMS ETOLL PH 131865 PARRAMATTA AUS Card xx3398 Value Date: 30/12/2014	10.00		$3,105.67 CR
02 Jan	THE GREENWOOD RESTAU NORTH SYDNEY NS	110.70		$2,994.97 CR
02 Jan	COTTON ON NORTH SYDNEY NS	102.45		$2,892.52 CR
03 Jan	KMART CHATSWOOD NSW AU	36.00		$2,856.52 CR
03 Jan	MADUNIT PTY LTD CHATSWOOD NSW	6.90		$2,849.62 CR
04 Jan	COLES CHATSWOOD NSW AU	26.05		$2,823.57 CR
04 Jan	Wdl ATM CBA ATM ARTARMON A NSW 2104	100.00		$2,723.57 CR
05 Jan	VODAFONE POSTPAID NetBank BPAY 52225 841942965	40.00		$2,683.57 CR
05 Jan	OPTUS BILLING NetBank BPAY 3061 90119477000183	145.00		$2,538.57 CR
06 Jan	Transfer to xx3403 NetBank	40.00		$2,498.57 CR
08 Jan	7-ELEVEN 2179 ARTARMON NS	15.00		$2,483.57 CR
08 Jan	Transfer to xx3403 NetBank	100.00		$2,383.57 CR
09 Jan	nab cards NetBank BPAY 1008 455702588691 9800 Cc pmt nab	120.00		$2,263.57 CR
09 Jan	Transfer to xx3403 NetBank	100.00		$2,163.57 CR
10 Jan	Transfer to other Bank NetBank Rent	1,112.00		$1,051.57 CR
10 Jan	MCDONALDS CREMORNE 0119 CREMORNE	5.50		$1,046.07 CR
10 Jan	HAYDEN THEATRES CREMORNE NSW	20.00		$1,026.07 CR
11 Jan	KMART CHATSWOOD NSW AU	3.50		$1,022.57 CR
11 Jan	KMART CHATSWOOD NSW AU	98.00		$924.57 CR
11 Jan	Refund Purchase KMART CHATSWOOD NSW AU		52.75	$977.32 CR
11 Jan	PLINE PH CHATSWOOD C0829 CHATSWOOD	9.17		$968.15 CR
12 Jan	TELSTRA CORP LTD NetBank BPAY 23796 2000149895210	100.37		$867.78 CR
12 Jan	Transfer to xx3403 NetBank	20.00		$847.78 CR
13 Jan	Transfer to xx3403 NetBank	40.00		$807.78 CR
13 Jan	Transfer to xx3403 NetBank	20.00		$787.78 CR
13 Jan	Salary RMS-PAYROLL WAGE/SA 00965493		3,145.93	$3,933.71 CR
14 Jan	Transfer to xx3403 NetBank	20.00		$3,913.71 CR
15 Jan	Transfer to xx3403 NetBank	80.00		$3,833.71 CR
15 Jan	OXFORD SHOP 103 9103 PARRAMATTA	51.60		$3,782.11 CR

Statement 22 (Page 8 of 13)

Account Number

Date	Transaction	Debit	Credit	Balance
15 Jan	GO COOL FRESH FRUIT HARRIS PARK AU	12.20		$3,769.91 CR
15 Jan	BP CONNECT 0999 PARRAMATTA AU	19.97		$3,749.94 CR
15 Jan	BROTHERS MEAT GROCERY EASTLAKES NSWAU	145.00		$3,604.94 CR
16 Jan	Transfer to xx3403 NetBank	40.00		$3,564.94 CR
16 Jan	HUDSONS COFFEE PARRAMATTA NSW	9.00		$3,555.94 CR
16 Jan	ecollect.com.au NetBank BPAY 30551 02021201 1450258 BBLAN5025	58.95		$3,496.99 CR
16 Jan	SUBWAY PARRAMATTA 0001 PARRAMATTA	5.95		$3,491.04 CR
16 Jan	PANCAKES ON THE ROCK0201 SYDNEY	75.25		$3,415.79 CR
17 Jan	Nick Logan Pharm Adv Artarmon AU	28.90		$3,386.89 CR
17 Jan	PIZZA HUT EXPRESS LANE COVE AU	16.85		$3,370.04 CR
19 Jan	Transfer to xx3403 NetBank	40.00		$3,330.04 CR
20 Jan	Transfer to xx3403 NetBank	20.00		$3,310.04 CR
21 Jan	Transfer to xx3403 NetBank	40.00		$3,270.04 CR
22 Jan	Transfer to xx3403 NetBank	100.00		$3,170.04 CR
23 Jan	Transfer to xx3403 NetBank	40.00		$3,130.04 CR
24 Jan	ALLIANZ INSURE C1 SYDNEY NS AUS Card xx3398 Value Date: 22/01/2015	96.58		$3,033.46 CR
24 Jan	Transfer to other Bank NetBank Rent	1,112.00		$1,921.46 CR
27 Jan	Transfer to xx0219 NetBank	160.00		$1,761.46 CR
27 Jan	Salary RMS-PAYROLL WAGE/SA 00965493		3,145.93	$4,907.39 CR
28 Jan	Transfer to xx3403 NetBank	60.00		$4,847.39 CR
28 Jan	Transfer to xx3403 NetBank	40.00		$4,807.39 CR
29 Jan	Transfer to xx3403 NetBank	60.00		$4,747.39 CR
29 Jan	Transfer to xx3403 NetBank	20.00		$4,727.39 CR
30 Jan	Transfer to xx3403 NetBank	20.00		$4,707.39 CR
31 Jan	Transfer to xx3403 NetBank	20.00		$4,687.39 CR
01 Feb	FAMILY NEEDS SUPERMA EASTLAKES NS	30.40		$4,656.99 CR
01 Feb	BROTHERS MEAT GROCERY EASTLAKES NSWAU	112.45		$4,544.54 CR
01 Feb	ALDI EASTLAKES AU	22.35		$4,522.19 CR
02 Feb	Transfer to xx3403 NetBank	50.00		$4,472.19 CR
03 Feb	Transfer to xx3403 NetBank	30.00		$4,442.19 CR
03 Feb	7-ELEVEN 2179 ARTARMON NS	18.98		$4,423.21 CR
04 Feb	7-ELEVEN 2173 ARTARMON NS	20.00		$4,403.21 CR
04 Feb	Transfer to xx3403 NetBank	20.00		$4,383.21 CR
04 Feb	Transfer to xx3403 NetBank	100.00		$4,283.21 CR
05 Feb	RMS ETOLL PH 131865 PARRAMATTA AUS Card xx3398 Value Date: 02/02/2015	10.00		$4,273.21 CR
05 Feb	Transfer to xx3403 NetBank	400.00		$3,873.21 CR
06 Feb	Direct Credit 012721 ATO ATO008000005796508		800.69	$4,673.90 CR
06 Feb	Transfer to xx3403 NetBank	40.00		$4,633.90 CR
06 Feb	Transfer to xx3403 NetBank	60.00		$4,573.90 CR

Date	Transaction	Debit	Credit	Balance
07 Feb	Direct Credit 015884 AUS GOV FAMILIES 841K6957281230356L		3,906.05	$8,479.95 CR
07 Feb	Direct Credit 015884 AUS GOV FAMILIES FB1K6957281230356L		354.05	$8,834.00 CR
07 Feb	Direct Credit 012721 ATO ATO006000005735106		224.69	$9,058.69 CR
07 Feb	Transfer to other Bank NetBank Rent	1,112.00		$7,946.69 CR
08 Feb	PRICELINE PHARM MACQ0873 NORTH RYDE	10.63		$7,936.06 CR
08 Feb	FOREVER 21 AU NORTH RYDE AU	16.90		$7,919.16 CR
08 Feb	J H MACQUARIE PTY LT NORTH RYDE NSW	15.00		$7,904.16 CR
08 Feb	ZARA AUSTRALIA 7089 NORTH RYDE	29.95		$7,874.21 CR
08 Feb	H&M HENNES & MAURITZ MACQUARIE PARNS	49.90		$7,824.31 CR
08 Feb	FOREVER 21 AU NORTH RYDE AU	23.80		$7,800.51 CR
08 Feb	ANDRE JEWELLERS WHOLNORTH RYDE AU	45.00		$7,755.51 CR
09 Feb	7-ELEVEN 2173 ARTARMON NS	20.00		$7,735.51 CR
09 Feb	Transfer to xx3403 NetBank	20.00		$7,715.51 CR
09 Feb	nab cards NetBank BPAY 1008 4557025686919800 payment	130.00		$7,585.51 CR
09 Feb	SUBWAY PARRAMATTA 0001 PARRAMATTA	6.20		$7,579.31 CR
09 Feb	Transfer to xx3403 NetBank	30.00		$7,549.31 CR
10 Feb	Transfer to xx3403 NetBank	20.00		$7,529.31 CR
10 Feb	OPTUS BILLING NetBank BPAY 3091 90119477000183	60.00		$7,469.31 CR
10 Feb	VODAFONE POSTPAID NetBank BPAY 52225 841942965	40.00		$7,429.31 CR
10 Feb	Salary RMS-PAYROLL WAGE/SA 00965493		3,145.94	$10,575.25 CR
10 Feb	Transfer to xx3403 NetBank	50.00		$10,525.25 CR
10 Feb	SEVEN COLOUR PTYLTD PARRAMATTA NSW	28.00		$10,497.25 CR
10 Feb	SES PARRAMATTAPARRAMATTA AU	52.97		$10,444.28 CR
11 Feb	Transfer to xx3403 NetBank	10.00		$10,434.28 CR
12 Feb	Transfer to xx3403 NetBank	30.00		$10,404.28 CR
12 Feb	CALTEX STARMART CHATSWOOD 28895 NSW Cash Out $30.00 Purchase $15.03	45.03		$10,359.25 CR
13 Feb	AUSTRALIAN MUSLIMS F MERRYLANDS W NSW	50.00		$10,309.25 CR
13 Feb	Transfer to xx3403 NetBank	40.00		$10,269.25 CR
14 Feb	CHELSEA GARDEN HOLDI ROSEBERY NS	16.90		$10,252.35 CR
14 Feb	Transfer to xx3403 NetBank	110.00		$10,142.35 CR
14 Feb	ALDI EASTLAKES AU	59.46		$10,082.89 CR
14 Feb	BROTHERS MEAT GROCERY EASTLAKES NSWAU	167.45		$9,915.44 CR
14 Feb	CALTEX WOOLWORTHS ROSEBERRY 22374 NSW	15.00		$9,900.44 CR
14 Feb	MEDICAL CTR PHARMC AU	15.95		$9,884.49 CR
15 Feb	KMART CHATSWOOD VIC AU	30.10		$9,854.39 CR
15 Feb	Wdl ATM CBA ATM CHATSWOOD CH 2 NSW 2844	20.00		$9,834.39 CR
15 Feb	MADUNIT PTY LTD CHATSWOOD NSW	6.90		$9,827.49 CR
16 Feb	Transfer to xx3403 NetBank	40.00		$9,787.49 CR

Statement 22 (Page 10 of 13)

Account Number

Date	Transaction	Debit	Credit	Balance
17 Feb	Transfer to xx3403 NetBank	20.00		$9,767.49 CR
17 Feb	ALDI 69 PARRAMATTA AU Cash Out $10.00 Purchase $13.00	23.00		$9,744.49 CR
18 Feb	SUBWAY PARRAMATTA 0031 PARRAMATTA	5.45		$9,739.04 CR
18 Feb	Transfer to xx3403 NetBank	15.00		$9,724.04 CR
18 Feb	CALTEX CARLINGFORD 22756 NSW	15.95		$9,708.09 CR
19 Feb	Transfer to xx3403 NetBank	30.00		$9,678.09 CR
20 Feb	7-ELEVEN 2173 ARTARMON NS Cash Out $19.00 Purchase $21.00	40.00		$9,638.09 CR
20 Feb	Wdl ATM CBA ATM PARRAMATTA B NSW 2223	40.00		$9,598.09 CR
20 Feb	Transfer to xx3403 NetBank	20.00		$9,578.09 CR
20 Feb	Wdl ATM CBA ATM ARTARMON A NSW 2104	20.00		$9,558.09 CR
21 Feb	7-ELEVEN 2179 ARTARMON NS	14.04		$9,544.05 CR
21 Feb	OPORTO TOP RYDE RYDE NS	10.86		$9,533.19 CR
21 Feb	Transfer to other Bank NetBank Rent	1,112.00		$8,421.19 CR
21 Feb	ACE MECHANICAL RPR TOP RYDE AU	228.50		$8,192.69 CR
22 Feb	Transfer to xx3403 NetBank	30.00		$8,162.69 CR
23 Feb	Transfer to xx3403 NetBank	30.00		$8,132.69 CR
23 Feb	Transfer to xx3403 NetBank	10.00		$8,122.69 CR
24 Feb	7-ELEVEN 2173 ARTARMON NS	40.00		$8,082.69 CR
24 Feb	Transfer to xx3403 NetBank	20.00		$8,062.69 CR
24 Feb	Wdl ATM CBA ATM ARTARMON A NSW 2104	40.00		$8,022.69 CR
24 Feb	Salary RMS-PAYROLL WAGE/SA 00965493		3,145.93	$11,168.62 CR
25 Feb	ALLIANZ INSURE C1 SYDNEY NS AUS Card xx3398 Value Date: 23/02/2015	96.58		$11,072.04 CR
25 Feb	CALTEX STARMART CHATSWOOD 28895 NSW	19.97		$11,052.07 CR
25 Feb	ESPRESSO BAR 101 PARRAMATTA NSW	18.70		$11,033.37 CR
25 Feb	Transfer to xx3403 NetBank	40.00		$10,993.37 CR
25 Feb	Transfer to xx3893 NetBank	10,000.00		$993.37 CR
25 Feb	ALDI 69 PARRAMATTA AU	9.47		$983.90 CR
25 Feb	Transfer to xx3403 NetBank	80.00		$903.90 CR
28 Feb	Wdl ATM CBA ATM ARTARMON A NSW 2104	20.00		$883.90 CR
01 Mar	Credit Interest		0.09	$883.99 CR
01 Mar	BP WILLOUGHBY 7240 WILLOUGHBY AU	15.00		$868.99 CR
01 Mar	7-ELEVEN 2173 ARTARMON NS Cash Out $15.00 Purchase $3.50	18.50		$850.49 CR
02 Mar	Transfer to xx3403 NetBank	45.00		$805.49 CR
03 Mar	Transfer to xx3403 NetBank	30.00		$775.49 CR
03 Mar	Wdl ATM CBA ATM PARRAMATTA C NSW 2223	20.00		$755.49 CR
03 Mar	Transfer to xx3403 NetBank	20.00		$735.49 CR
04 Mar	Transfer to xx3403 NetBank	20.00		$715.49 CR
05 Mar	Transfer to xx3403 NetBank	20.00		$695.49 CR
05 Mar	Transfer to xx3403 NetBank	15.00		$680.49 CR
06 Mar	Transfer to xx3403 NetBank	15.00		$665.49 CR

Statement 22 (Page 11 of 13)

Account Number

Date	Transaction	Debit	Credit	Balance
07 Mar	Transfer to xx3403 NetBank	20.00		$645.49 CR
07 Mar	Transfer from xx3893 NetBank Rent		1,112.00	$1,757.49 CR
07 Mar	Transfer to other Bank NetBank Rent	1,112.00		$645.49 CR
09 Mar	OPTUS BILLING NetBank BPAY 3061 90119477000183	120.00		$525.49 CR
09 Mar	Transfer to xx3403 NetBank	50.00		$475.49 CR
09 Mar	Transfer to xx3403 NetBank	20.00		$455.49 CR
10 Mar	Transfer to xx3403 NetBank	25.00		$430.49 CR
10 Mar	SUBWAY SMITH ST PARRAMATTANSWAU	6.20		$424.29 CR
10 Mar	Transfer to xx3403 NetBank	25.00		$399.29 CR
10 Mar	Salary RMS-PAYROLL WAGE/SA 00965493		3,145.94	$3,545.23 CR
10 Mar	7-ELEVEN 2128 CARLINGFORD NS	15.20		$3,530.03 CR
11 Mar	Transfer to xx3403 NetBank	20.00		$3,510.03 CR
11 Mar	Transfer to xx3403 NetBank	20.00		$3,490.03 CR
11 Mar	KMART CHATSWOOD VIC AU	10.00		$3,480.03 CR
11 Mar	COLES CHATSWOOD CHASE NSW AU	112.21		$3,367.82 CR
13 Mar	Transfer to xx3403 NetBank	250.00		$3,117.82 CR
13 Mar	ALDI 69 PARRAMATTA AU	35.31		$3,082.51 CR
13 Mar	PARRAMATTA VI	10.83		$3,071.68 CR
14 Mar	Wdl ATM CUSS DAY & NIGHT CHEMISNEWTOWN	20.00		$3,051.68 CR
14 Mar	Non CBA ATM Withdrawal Fee	2.50		$3,049.18 CR
14 Mar	ASAKUSA IN NEWTOWN NEWTOWN NSWAU	70.70		$2,978.48 CR
15 Mar	MAX BRENNER NEWTOWN AU	14.70		$2,963.78 CR
15 Mar	7-ELEVEN 2179 ARTARMON NS	46.01		$2,917.77 CR
15 Mar	ALDI EASTLAKES AU	60.81		$2,856.96 CR
15 Mar	BROTHERS MEAT GROCERY EASTLAKES NSWAU	154.45		$2,702.51 CR
16 Mar	Transfer to xx3403 NetBank	20.00		$2,682.51 CR
16 Mar	Transfer to xx3403 NetBank	25.00		$2,657.51 CR
16 Mar	Transfer to xx3403 NetBank	100.00		$2,557.51 CR
17 Mar	EMERI COKISZELA CHATSWOOD NSW	40.00		$2,517.51 CR
18 Mar	SUBWAY PARRAMATTA 0001 PARRAMATTA	5.45		$2,512.06 CR
18 Mar	EnergyAustralia Pty NetBank BPAY 97410 10029776998426	150.00		$2,362.06 CR
18 Mar	Transfer to xx3403 NetBank	20.00		$2,342.06 CR
18 Mar	Transfer from xx3893 NetBank pmt		250.00	$2,592.06 CR
18 Mar	Transfer to xx0219 NetBank pmt	250.00		$2,342.06 CR
19 Mar	RMS ETOLL PH 131865 PARRAMATTA AUS Card xx3398 Value Date: 15/03/2015	10.00		$2,332.06 CR
19 Mar	Transfer to xx3403 NetBank	20.00		$2,312.06 CR
19 Mar	7-ELEVEN 2085 PARRAMATTA NS	20.00		$2,292.06 CR
19 Mar	Transfer to xx3403 NetBank	20.00		$2,272.06 CR

Statement 22 (Page 12 of 13)

Account Number

Date	Transaction	Debit	Credit	Balance
19 Mar	Transfer to xx3403 NetBank	25.00		$2,247.06 CR
20 Mar	7-ELEVEN 2173 ARTARMON NS Cash Out $15.00 Purchase $20.00	35.00		$2,212.06 CR
20 Mar	ALDI 73 CHATSWOOD AU	11.36		$2,200.70 CR
21 Mar	Transfer to other Bank NetBank Rent	1,184.00		$1,016.70 CR
21 Mar	EMERICO KISZELA CHATSWOOD NSW	20.00		$996.70 CR
22 Mar	TELSTRA CORP LTD NetBank BPAY 23796 2000149885210	60.00		$936.70 CR
23 Mar	CALTEX STARMART CHATSWOOD 28895 NSW	20.02		$916.68 CR
23 Mar	Transfer to xx3403 NetBank	30.00		$886.68 CR
23 Mar	VODAFONE POSTPAID NetBank BPAY 52225 841942985	40.00		$846.68 CR
23 Mar	Wdl ATM CBA ATM ASHFIELD B NSW 2105	20.00		$826.68 CR
24 Mar	7-ELEVEN 2243 LINDFIELD NS	21.00		$805.68 CR
24 Mar	GUZMAN Y GOMEZ WESTF PARRAMATTA NSW	8.50		$797.18 CR
24 Mar	Salary RMS-PAYROLL WAGE/SA 00965493		3,145.93	$3,943.11 CR
25 Mar	ALLIANZ INSURE C1 SYDNEY NS AUS Card xx3396 Value Date: 23/03/2015	96.58		$3,846.53 CR
25 Mar	Transfer to xx3403 NetBank	20.00		$3,826.53 CR
25 Mar	ESPRESSO BAR 101 PARRAMATTA NSW	6.20		$3,820.33 CR
25 Mar	SUBWAY PARRAMATTA 0001 PARRAMATTA	6.20		$3,814.13 CR
25 Mar	Transfer to xx3403 NetBank	50.00		$3,764.13 CR
25 Mar	ALDI 69 PARRAMATTA AU	41.00		$3,723.13 CR
27 Mar	Transfer to xx3403 NetBank	20.00		$3,703.13 CR
27 Mar	ALDI 69 PARRAMATTA AU	8.72		$3,694.41 CR
28 Mar	ALDI 73 CHATSWOOD AU	58.46		$3,635.95 CR
28 Mar	MIRACLE WCW CHATSWOOD AU	18.40		$3,617.55 CR
28 Mar	FRUTESH CHATSWOOD NSW2	13.44		$3,604.11 CR
28 Mar	FARM FRESH MEATS 1601 CHATSWOOD	16.30		$3,587.81 CR
29 Mar	7-ELEVEN 2179 ARTARMON NS	23.00		$3,564.81 CR
29 Mar	BROTHERS MEAT GROCERY EASTLAKES NSWAU	114.20		$3,450.61 CR
30 Mar	Transfer to xx3403 NetBank	30.00		$3,420.61 CR
30 Mar	Transfer to xx0219 NetBank pmt	165.00		$3,255.61 CR
30 Mar	Transfer to xx0219 NetBank visa	265.00		$2,990.61 CR
30 Mar	COLES CHATSWOOD VIC AU	58.33		$2,932.28 CR
30 Mar	Wdl ATM CBA ATM WF CHATSWOOD 3 NSW 2140	40.00		$2,892.28 CR
31 Mar	CALTEX STARMART CHATSWOOD 28895 NSW	20.99		$2,871.29 CR
31 Mar	PARRAMATTA EASY MART PARRAMATTA NSW	30.00		$2,841.29 CR

Statement 22 (Page 13 of 13)

Account Number

Date	Transaction	Debit	Credit	Balance
31 Mar	MCDONALDS WYNYARD RA0493 SYDNEY	8.45		$2,832.84 CR
31 Mar 2015	CLOSING BALANCE			$2,832.84 CR

Opening balance	−	Total debits	+	Total credits	=	Closing balance
$1,915.82 CR		$77,872.35		$78,789.37		$2,832.84 CR

Transaction Summary during 1st October 2014 to 31st March 2015

Transaction Type	01 Oct to 30 Nov	01 Dec to 31 Jan	01 Feb to 31 Mar	Free	Chargeable	Unit Price	Fee Charged
Staff assisted withdrawals	1	0	0	0	1	$0.00	$0.00
Cheques written	0	0	0	0	0	$0.00	$0.00
Total	1	0	0	0	1		$0.00
Account Fee						$0.00	$0.00

Effective Wednesday 30 September 2015, the Transaction, Savings and Investment Accounts Terms and Conditions dated 12 March 2014, are amended as follows:

- The *Complete Home Loan* monthly account fee and/or withdrawal fee exemption is being replaced with the *Home Loan everyday account fee* exemption. If you have a current home loan (excluding Viridian Line of Credit and Equity Unlock Loan for Seniors) that you own either individually or jointly in personal name/s, we will exempt your monthly account fee on eligible transaction, savings and investment accounts. Eligible accounts are Smart Access, Complete Access, Streamline, Commonwealth Direct Investment Account, Cash Investment Account and Cash Management Call Account.

- The *Relationship Balance* exemption is being simplified. If you have a total of $50,000 or more in your eligible contributing accounts that you own either individually or jointly, we will waive your monthly account fee (MAF) and/or withdrawal fee (WF), on eligible transaction, savings and investment accounts which are in an individual or joint name. Your Relationship Balance is automatically calculated on the 2nd last day of each month. If the total amount in your eligible contributing accounts falls below $50,000 at the time the Relationship Balance is calculated, your MAF and/or WF will not be waived on eligible transaction, savings and investment accounts which are in an individual or joint name. Eligible contributing accounts are Accelerator Cash Account, Award Saver Account, Cash Investment Account, Cash Management Call Account, Complete Access, Commonwealth Direct Investment Account, Farm Management Deposit, GoalSaver Account, NetBank Saver, Passbook Savings Account, Private Banking Account, Savings Investment Account, Smart Access, Streamline Account, Term Deposit and Viridian Line of Credit. Transaction, savings and investments accounts eligible for Relationship Balance and the fees that will be exempted (MAF and/or WF) are unchanged.

- If you complete a Maestro (EFTPOS) or Debit MasterCard purchase in Australian dollars when overseas, an *International transaction fee* equivalent to 3.00% of the transaction value will apply.

You can get a copy of the Terms and Conditions from our website at www.commbank.com.au by calling us or visiting any branch.

Resume or Curriculum Vitae

Licensed Geotechnical Engineer

4/3 Elizabeth Street • Artarmon • NSW 2064
0402-730-410 (mobile) • 9419-8605 (home)
gmail.com (personal) • rms.nsw.gov.au (work)

GENERAL PROFILE

Senior Civil (geotechnical) engineer with experiences in a variety of infrastructure, residential/commercial, ground improvement and hillside related projects. Strong verbal and written communication skills gained in current and previous senior technical roles. Experienced in project management using PMBOK key knowledge areas in delivering code compliant projects within cost and budget. Extensive engineering work experience in highly seismic west coast of the United States. Detailed knowledge of various Australian building codes gained through involvement in infrastructure related projects in a senior level. Proven experience in collaboration and management of technical teams.

Specific geotechnical experiences include planning and supervision of site investigations, geotechnical laboratory testing, site classification assessments, shallow and deep foundation capacity analysis including rock foundations, settlement analysis, pile lateral capacity assessment, soil and rock slope stability assessments and slip mitigation design with ground anchors, soil nails and rock bolts, earth retention system design including gravity walls, RSW walls, ground anchored walls and soil nail walls, ground improvement designs such as CMC piles, jet grouting, stone columns, wick drains, and specialty micropiles.

QUALIFICATION SUMMARY

- I have experience in seismic projects related to liquefaction assessments, lateral spread, and seismic slope stability analysis gained in various civil engineering projects in California, USA.
- I have in-depth knowledge of various Australian building codes gained through my involvement in some high profile civil engineering and infrastructure projects with reputable companies and government agency.
- I am currently an engineering official for the Transport department of NSW government, Australia. I routinely liaise with consulting engineers in communicating technical issues.
- I have analysis experience with a large number of industry-standard software.
- I have project & team management experience.

ENGINEERING SOFTWARE EXPERIENCE

SOFTWARE SPECIFIC EXPERIENCE

WALLAP	I have used this software to determine bending moment, shear, and deflection of sheet piles, piled walls, concrete walls with anchors. I have also used it to compute single pile lateral capacity for piled wall systems.
PLAXIS	I have used PLAXIS to undertake FEM analysis of foundation settlement, deflection of temporary retaining walls with anchors, ground improvement analysis (controlled modulus columns), ground settlement due to underboring and tunnelling and other serviceability computations.
SLOPE W	I have used Slope W to perform limit equilibrium slope stability analysis for embankment slopes, retaining wall overall stability including soil nail walls, and stability analysis of slopes over improved ground.
SLIDE	I have used this software as an alternate for SLOPE W to perform limit equilibrium analysis.
L-Pile	I have used L-pile to undertake single pile lateral capacity analysis.
GROUP	I have used GROUP for pile group lateral capacity and loading analysis, including micropiles.
Settle3D	I have used this software to compute consolidation settlement of shallow foundations for residential and commercial projects.
MathCAD	I have programmed with MathCAD for soil nail wall facing design, micro pile capacity assessment, retaining wall stability analysis, ground anchor loading assessment, and shallow foundation elastic settlement analysis.

SOFTWARE SPECIFIC EXPERIENCE

EXCEL VBA	I am well versed in programming with EXCEL Visual Basic for Applications platform. I have written VBA programmes for foundation elastic settlement, ground anchor load assessment, computation of bending moment in Micropiles, lateral spread during liquefaction, subsurface stresses under footing, effect of surcharge on retention systems, temporary shoring design etc.
LiquefyPro	I used this software extensively to assess liquefaction potential using both SPT and CPT methods.
Microsoft Project	I have used this software in managing larger engineering projects for preparation of task lists and Gantt charts.

I also have working knowledge of GRLWEAP (pile driving wave analysis) and Repute (pile lateral capacity analysis).

CODES AND STANDARDS KNOWLEDGE

Due to my work experience in Australia and the USA, I have gained in-depth knowledge of building codes from both countries. A short list of the codes and specifications is provided below.

Engineering Topic	Code
Residential site classification, footing and design	Australian AS 2870 British Standard BS 8004
Earth Retention Systems	Australian AS4678, Australian AS 5100.3 (General) RMS R56, FHWA-IF-99-015, BS 8081 (Ground Anchors) RMS R57, BS 8006, FHWA-NHI-10-024 (RSW Walls) RMS R64, FHWA-SA-96-069R (Soil Nailing)
Piles Rock Socketed Shafts, Micropiles	Australian AS2159, California Building code FHWA-SA97-070 (Micropiles)
Earthworks	Australian AS 3798, RMS R44, California Building code

CAREER HISTORY

Following is a list of employers that I have worked for in the last 14 years as a Geotechnical Engineer.

Employer-Role	Duration	General Responsibilities
Roads & Maritimes Services, TfNSW, Sydney, Australia – Geotechnical Engineer	2013-Present	Be part of design process of various infrastructure projects within the RMS Asset Maintenance section. Communicate, collaborate and assist internal (RMS project managers) and external stakeholders in the design process, review and monitoring for successful outcomes for asset maintenance and other infrastructure projects. Provide engineering recommendations. Undertake review of submitted engineering plans and geotechnical reports for conformance with project SWTC and applicable codes in project risk management, provide high level customer service to both internal and external stakeholders by completing assigned work within time and budget. Assist in contract and scope of works preparation. Technical report preparation and engineering analysis.
Keller Ground Engineering Australia, Sydney, Australia-Geotechnical Design Manager	2012-2013	Management of engineering portion of civil engineering projects. Assist in project scoping, cost estimations, & contract preparation. Manage engineering team design activities. High level verbal and written communication with internal (engineer, drafting officer) and external (Council engineer, structural engineer) stakeholders in completing engineering design and review process. Construction oversight for piling, ground improvement works etc. Technical report and construction drawing preparation. Assist and coach junior engineers.
Hyder Consulting, Sydney, Australia-Senior Geotechnical Engineer	2010-2012	Using PMBOK key knowledge areas to manage a technical team within the design group for the construction of a major highway project (2010-2011). Manage a technical team to deliver design and reports for more than 30 retaining

Employer-Role	Duration	General Responsibilities
		structures by undertaking the following 1) scope management b) design integration c) budget management d) deliverables management e) extensive verbal and written communication with internal and external stakeholders in design and review.
Terracosta Consulting Inc., Los Angeles, California, USA – Senior Geotechnical Engineer	2006-2009	Manage design portion of civil engineering and infrastructure projects by undertaking 1) scoping of projects 2) complete and assist in contract preparation c) lead technical teams, provide technical guidance, manage billing hours d) assist in project billing management e) extensive verbal and written communication with various stakeholders in design, review and monitoring of engineering projects f) undertake engineering design, plan preparation, and technical report writing.
Subsurface Designs Inc., Los Angeles, California, USA – Geotechnical Engineer	2005-2006	Manage investigation, design and reporting process of various civil engineering projects by undertaking 1) plan and supervise engineering site investigations 2) sub-contractor management 3) prepare and assist in preparation of contracts 4) engineering analysis and reporting 5) extensive technical written and verbal communication with various internal (engineers, laboratory technician) and external stakeholders (council engineers, architects, design engineers). Attend engineering training.
Ralph Stone & Company, Inc., Los Angeles, California, USA – Geotechnical Engineer	2001-2005	Geotechnical site investigations, sampling, geotechnical laboratory testing for soil strength, compressibility, particle size distribution, clay plasticity, compaction characteristics, geotechnical assessment of soil and rock slopes, foundation capacity, settlement, liquefaction, lateral spreading potential, technical report writing.

EDUCATION

Bachelor of Science Degree in Civil Engineering (BSCE), California State University, Long Beach, California, USA – 2001 (successfully assessed to an equivalent 4-year Australian engineering degree).

Candidate for Masters in Geotechnical Engineering degree, University of New South Wales, Sydney, Australia. Expected completion: 2015-2016.

CHARTERSHIP

Registered Professional Engineer (PE-USA) #70510, California Board of Professional Engineers and Land Surveyors – 2006.

REFERENCES

1. Oliver Batchelor, National General Manager, Keller Ground Engineering (KGE) Australia, Sydney, Australia ♦ Phone: +61 (02) 8866-1155.
2. Dr David Salter, Principal, DRS Engineering Inc., Los Angeles, CA, USA ♦ Phone: 1-818 402 3962.

SAMPLE PROJECT LIST

A sample list of projects related to the requirements of the applied position.

Company/Position	PROJECT	Involvement Duration	Project Description
Ralph Stone and Company – Staff Geotechnical Engineer	Veragua Road residential development, Playa Del Rey, Los Angeles, CA, USA	March 2003-June 2003	Project Description: Multi-level residential mansion development in a highly seismic sloping lot with liquefaction potential. Duties: Plan and arrange site investigation, subsurface sampling, preparation of logs, planning laboratory testing and review of test results, engineering analysis including seismic slope stability, pile lateral capacity analysis, basement design, earthworks, technical report writing, extensive communication with project engineering geologist, City officials.
Ralph Stone and Company	Abbott Kinney apartment	February 2004- June	Project Description: Multi-storey, multi-family residential development in highly seismic zone with liquefaction potential.

– Staff Geotechnical Engineer	development, Venice area, Los Angeles, CA, USA	2004	Duties: Plan and arrange site investigation, subsurface sampling, preparation of logs, planning laboratory testing and review of test results, engineering analysis including seismic slope stability, pile lateral capacity analysis, basement design, earthworks, technical report writing, extensive communication with project engineering geologist, City officials.
Subsurface Designs Inc. – Project Geotechnical Engineer	Residential Tract Geotechnical Investigation, Ventura County, California (US $6million+)	May 2005-September 2005	Project Description: Residential tract development in highly seismic site with liquefaction potential. Duties: Geotechnical site investigation, liquefaction analysis, foundation and earthworks recommendation for residential tract comprising 18 single family residences. My responsibilities included undertaking geotechnical site investigations with mechanical drilling and test pitting for liquefaction and foundation capacity assessments, and earthworks. I supervised drilling with SPT sampling, CPTs and test pitting, assigned laboratory testing, undertook liquefaction analysis with LiquefyPro, prepared foundation settlement analysis using EXCEL spreadsheets, prepared geotechnical report, and responded to review comments by City officials.
Terracosta Consulting Inc. – Project Geotechnical Engineer	Golden State Water Company Slope failure remediation, Los Angeles, California (US $50 million+)	September 2008-July 2009	Project Description: Slope failure remediation work at water tank site owned by State Utility. Duties: responsibilities included design and analysis of remediation system comprising soil nails with concrete facing and steel mesh with anchors. I used MathCAD to write structural capacity design of concrete face, Slide™ to determine failure surface and nail length, and used AutoCAD to prepare construction plans for submission. During feasibility stages, I prepared and presented design solution to the Principal's design and review team. I also attended pre-construction meetings, and provided other technical support to the Contractor. Construction of the project commenced in late 2009.
Hyder Consulting Inc. – Senior Geotechnical Engineer	Hunter Expressway Alliance, Hunter Region NSW (AUD $870million)	April 2010-January 2012	Project Description: 9km long highway design and construction in Central Coast, NSW, Australia. Duties: Team management and deliver of critical design elements using the PMBOK key knowledge areas, project scope assessment, team budget and human resource management, deliverables management by maintaining key dates, delivery formats and quality control checks, design integration management by obtaining and providing engineering inputs and outputs, mentoring and coaching junior team engineers, report preparation, WH&S report preparation and review, Safety in Design meeting management and assistance, Risk assessment of design elements etc.
Keller Ground Engineering – Geotechnical Design Manager	HMAS Platypus Site environmental Remediation (AUD $50 mil+)	June 2012-February 2013	Project Description: Environmental cleaning of hazardous site requiring temporary earth retention and hydraulic barrier construction Duties: Assist in project scoping, undertake design of temporary retention system and hydraulic barrier by jet grouting, technical reporting and construction plan preparation with AutoCAD and MathCAD, extensive liaison with project contractor and council representatives, construction oversight.
Keller Ground Engineering – Geotechnical Design Manager	Institute of Marine and Antarctic Studies, Hobart, Tasmania (AUD $5mil+)	April 2012-Nov 2012	Project Description: support of two storey IMAS centre using micropiles. Duties: Design capacity assessment of micropile using FHWA method. I wrote EXCEL program with VBA to analysis pile design capacity and pile cap shear capacity analysis. I undertook micropile lateral capacity analysis using GROUP™. I prepared technical report, construction plan with AutoCAD, responded to review comments, attended meetings with Architect and Structural Engineer in Hobart, assisted Keller construction team with technical questions. Project completed in Nov 2012.
RMS – Geotechnical	Wynyard Walkway	June 2013-Present	Project: Tunnel works spanning from Darling Harbour to Wynyard Station

| Engineer | Pedestrian Tunnel - Sydney (Cost AUD $100 million+) | Duties: Review of geotechnical ground modelling, tunnel primary and permanent lining design, temporary ground anchors. Also reviewed tunnelling monitoring plan and monitoring reports, review of non-conformance reports, extensive verbal and written communication with various internal and external stakeholders. |

Signed Statement of Intent to Depart

April 20, 2015

U.S. Consulate General, Sydney
Level 10, MLC Centre
19-29 Martin Place
Sydney, NSW 2000

    Re: E-2 Treaty Investor
           Petitioner: RK Engineering Works, Inc.
           Beneficiary/Applicant: New Applicant

To Whom It May Concern:

This letter is to confirm that it is my full intention to depart the United States and return to the Australia upon expiration of any E-2 status granted to me.

Sincerely,

Articles of Incorporation

ARTS-GS	**Articles of Incorporation of a General Stock Corporation**

To form a general stock corporation in California, you can fill out this form or prepare your own document, and submit for filing along with:

- A $100 filing fee.
- A separate, non-refundable $15 service fee also must be included, if you drop off the completed form or document.

Important! Corporations in California may have to pay a minimum $800 yearly tax to the California Franchise Tax Board. For more information, go to https://www.ftb.ca.gov.

Note: Before submitting the completed form, you should consult with a private attorney for advice about your specific business needs.

This Space For Office Use Only

For questions about this form, go to www.sos.ca.gov/business/be/filing-tips.htm

Corporate Name (List the proposed corporate name. Go to www.sos.ca.gov/business/be/name-availability.htm for general corporate name requirements and restrictions.)

① The name of the corporation is ███████████

Corporate Purpose

② The purpose of the corporation is to engage in any lawful act or activity for which a corporation may be organized under the General Corporation Law of California other than the banking business, the trust company business or the practice of a profession permitted to be incorporated by the California Corporations Code.

Service of Process (List a California resident or a California registered corporate agent that agrees to be your initial agent to accept service of process in case your corporation is sued. You may list any adult who lives in California. You may not list your own corporation as the agent. Do not list an address if the agent is a California registered corporate agent as the address for service of process is already on file.)

③ a. ███████████
   Agent's Name

   b. _____
   Agent's Street Address (if agent is not a corporation) - Do not list a P.O. Box   *City (no abbreviations)*   *State*   *Zip*

Corporate Addresses

④ a. ███████████   ███████   ████
   Initial Street Address of Corporation - Do not list a P.O. Box   *City (no abbreviations)*   *State*   *Zip*

   b. _____
   Initial Mailing Address of Corporation, if different from 4a   *City (no abbreviations)*   *State*   *Zip*

Shares (List the number of shares the corporation is authorized to issue. Note: Before shares of stock are sold or issued, the corporation must comply with the Corporate Securities Law of 1968 administered by the California Department of Business Oversight. For more information, go to www.dbo.ca.gov or call the California Department of Business Oversight at (866) 275-2677.)

⑤ This corporation is authorized to issue only one class of shares of stock.
The total number of shares which this corporation is authorized to issue is ____10____

This form must be signed by each incorporator. If you need more space, attach extra pages that are 1-sided and on standard letter-sized paper (8 1/2" x 11"). All attachments are made part of these articles of incorporation.

███
Incorporator - Sign here   *Print your name here*

Make check/money order payable to: Secretary of State	By Mail	Drop-Off
Upon filing, we will return one (1) uncertified copy of your filed document for free, and will certify the copy upon request and payment of a $5 certification fee.	Secretary of State Business Entities, P.O. Box 944260 Sacramento, CA 94244-2600	Secretary of State 1500 11th Street, 3rd Floor Sacramento, CA 95814

Corporations Code §§ 200-202 et seq.; Revenue and Taxation Code § 23153
ARTS-GS (REV 03/2014)

2014 California Secretary of State
www.sos.ca.gov/business/be

Statement of Information

14-071662

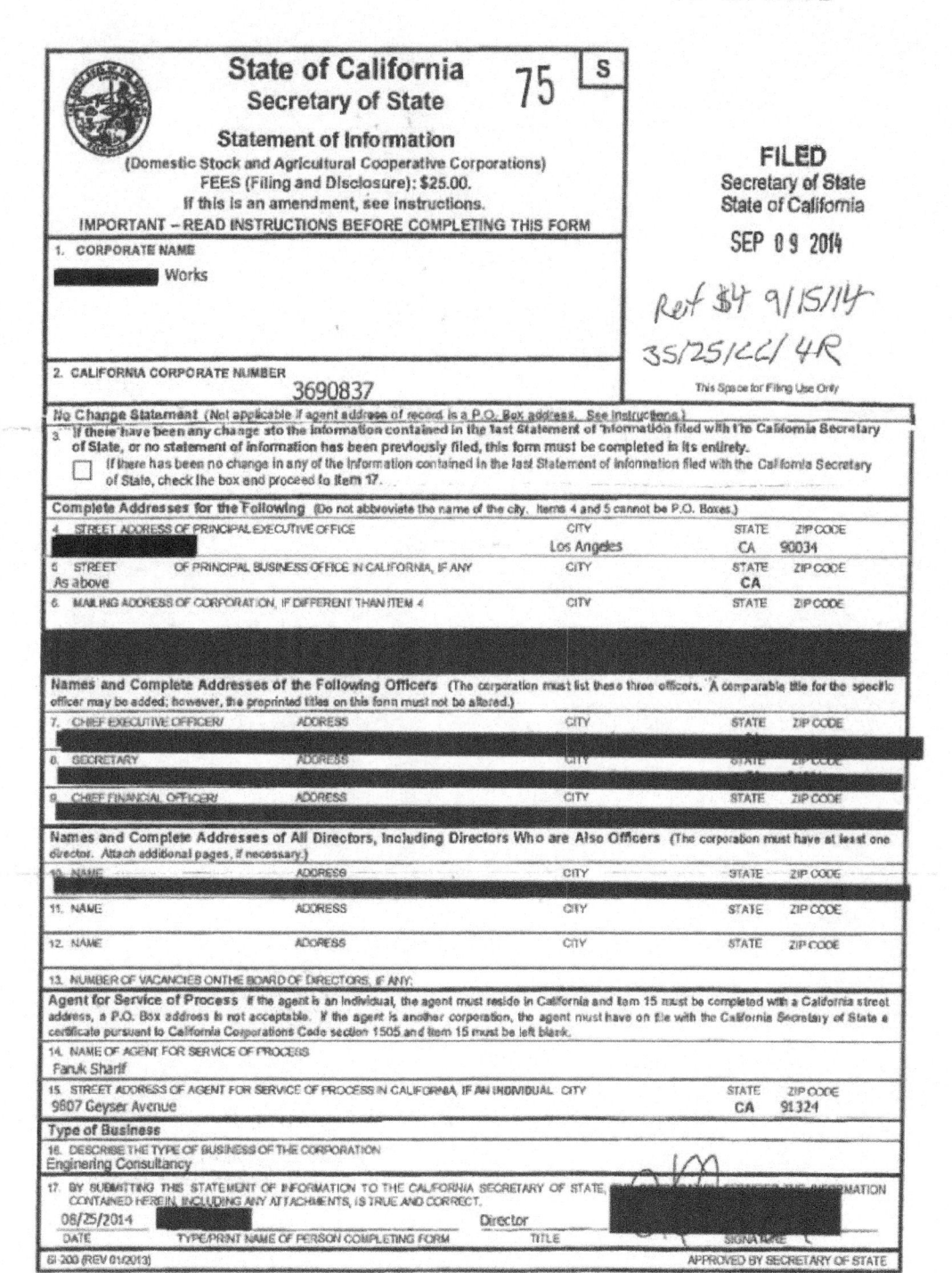

State of California
Secretary of State
Statement of Information
(Domestic Stock and Agricultural Cooperative Corporations)
FEES (Filing and Disclosure): $25.00.
If this is an amendment, see instructions.
IMPORTANT – READ INSTRUCTIONS BEFORE COMPLETING THIS FORM

75 S

FILED
Secretary of State
State of California

SEP 09 2014

Ref $4 9/15/14
35/25/CC/4R

This Space for Filing Use Only

1. CORPORATE NAME
███ Works

2. CALIFORNIA CORPORATE NUMBER
3690837

No Change Statement (Not applicable if agent address of record is a P.O. Box address. See instructions.)
3. If there have been any changes to the information contained in the last Statement of Information filed with the California Secretary of State, or no statement of information has been previously filed, this form must be completed in its entirety.
☐ If there has been no change in any of the information contained in the last Statement of Information filed with the California Secretary of State, check the box and proceed to Item 17.

Complete Addresses for the Following (Do not abbreviate the name of the city. Items 4 and 5 cannot be P.O. Boxes.)

		CITY	STATE	ZIP CODE
4. STREET ADDRESS OF PRINCIPAL EXECUTIVE OFFICE	███	Los Angeles	CA	90034
5. STREET OF PRINCIPAL BUSINESS OFFICE IN CALIFORNIA, IF ANY	As above	CITY	CA	ZIP CODE
6. MAILING ADDRESS OF CORPORATION, IF DIFFERENT THAN ITEM 4		CITY	STATE	ZIP CODE

Names and Complete Addresses of the Following Officers (The corporation must list these three officers. A comparable title for the specific officer may be added; however, the preprinted titles on this form must not be altered.)

	ADDRESS	CITY	STATE	ZIP CODE
7. CHIEF EXECUTIVE OFFICER/				
8. SECRETARY				
9. CHIEF FINANCIAL OFFICER/				

Names and Complete Addresses of All Directors, Including Directors Who are Also Officers (The corporation must have at least one director. Attach additional pages, if necessary.)

	ADDRESS	CITY	STATE	ZIP CODE
10. NAME				
11. NAME				
12. NAME				

13. NUMBER OF VACANCIES ON THE BOARD OF DIRECTORS, IF ANY:

Agent for Service of Process If the agent is an individual, the agent must reside in California and Item 15 must be completed with a California street address, a P.O. Box address is not acceptable. If the agent is another corporation, the agent must have on file with the California Secretary of State a certificate pursuant to California Corporations Code section 1505 and Item 15 must be left blank.

14. NAME OF AGENT FOR SERVICE OF PROCESS
Faruk Sharif

15. STREET ADDRESS OF AGENT FOR SERVICE OF PROCESS IN CALIFORNIA, IF AN INDIVIDUAL — CITY — STATE — ZIP CODE
9807 Geyser Avenue — CA — 91324

Type of Business
16. DESCRIBE THE TYPE OF BUSINESS OF THE CORPORATION
Engineering Consultancy

17. BY SUBMITTING THIS STATEMENT OF INFORMATION TO THE CALIFORNIA SECRETARY OF STATE, ███ INFORMATION CONTAINED HEREIN, INCLUDING ANY ATTACHMENTS, IS TRUE AND CORRECT.

08/25/2014	███	Director	███
DATE	TYPE/PRINT NAME OF PERSON COMPLETING FORM	TITLE	SIGNATURE

SI-200 (REV 01/2013) — APPROVED BY SECRETARY OF STATE

PAGE 53

Incorporator
Organizational Action

RK ENGINEERING WORKS
A California Corporation
████████████
Los Angeles, CA 90034

INCORPORATOR ORGANIZATIONAL ACTION
OF
████████ WORKS, INC.
SEPTEMBER 1ST 2014

The undersigned, being the sole Incorporator of ████████ Works, Inc. a California Corporation (the "Company"), hereby adopts the following resolutions pursuant to Section 210 of the General Corporation Law of California with respect to the initial organization of the corporation:

1. Adoption of Article of Incorporation

RESOLVED: That the Certificate of Incorporation attached hereto as Exhibit A (the "Article of Incorporation"), be, and hereby is, adopted as the Article of Incorporation for the Corporation and that the Article of Incorporation be filed with the California Secretary of State.

2. Adoption of Bylaws

RESOLVED: That the Bylaws attached hereto as Exhibit B are hereby adopted as the Bylaws for the Corporation.

3. Resignation of the Sole Incorporator

RESOLVED: That the undersigned, being the Sole Incorporator of the Corporation, having taken all actions necessary and appropriate in connection with the incorporation of the Corporation, does hereby tender the undersigned's resignation as the Sole Incorporator to the Board of Directors as constituted above.

4. Sale of Common Stock

RESOLVED: That the directors and officers are authorized to sell and issue on behalf of the Company Common Stock (the "Shares") to the individuals or entities listed below (the "Purchasers") in the amounts as specified or agreed upon by the directors and officers of the said company and the individuals and entities listed below:

Shareholder	Number of Shares	Total Consideration
██████████	5	$50,000

RESOLVED: That, upon payment of the consideration the Common Stock shall be duly and validly issued, fully paid and non-assessable.

RESOLVED: To authorize the proper officers of the Company to execute and deliver certificates for the number of shares of Common Stock so subscribed and paid for.

RESOLVED: That it is desirable and in the best interest of the Company that the sale and issuance of shares of Common stock, be qualified or registered or exempted from qualification or registration in various states and under federal securities laws; that the officers of the Company be, and each of them acting singly hereby is, authorized and directed, in the name and on behalf of the Company, to determine the states in which appropriate officers or officer may deem advisable; that such officers or officer hereby are authorized to perform, on behalf of the Company and its name, any and all such acts as any such officers or officer may deem necessary or advisable in order to comply with the applicable federal laws and applicable laws of any such states, and in connection therewith, to execute and file all requisite papers and documents, including, but not limited to, applications, report, surety bonds, irrevocable consents and appointments of attorneys for service in process; and that the execution by any such officer or officers of any such paper or document or the doing by any of them of any act in connection with the foregoing matters shall conclusively establish their authority therefor from the Company and the approval and ratification of the Company of the papers and documents so executed and the action so taken.

RESOLVED: That if the securities or "Blue Sky" laws of any of the states in which the officers or an officer of the Company deem it necessary or advisable to qualify or register or exempt from qualification or registration the sale and issuance of the share of Common stock, or to register the Company as a dealer or broker, or any authority administering such laws, require or requires a prescribed form of preamble, resolution or resolutions, or consent to service of process in connection with such sale or issuance, each such preamble, resolution or consent is hereby adopted by the Board and the officers of the Company be, and each of them acting singly hereby is, authorized and directed, in the name and on behalf of the Company, to certify the adoption of such preamble, resolution or consent.

5. Election of Directors

RESOLVED: That, the following individual is hereby appointed as director of the Company, to serve as the director until his/her successor is duly elected and qualified:

DIRECTOR: ███

6. Election of Officers

RESOLVED: That, the following individuals are hereby appointed as officers of the Company, each to hold the office set forth opposite his/her name until his/her successor is duly elected and qualified, or until such officer sooner dies, resign, is removed or becomes disqualified:

PRESIDENT: ███
SECRETARY: ███
TREASURER: ███

RESOLVED: That that Statement of Information form SI-200 attached hereto as Exhibit B, is hereby adopted as the Statement of Information, and that a completed Statement of Information is to be filed with the office of the California Secretary of State.

7. Form of Common Stock Certificate

RESOLVED: That the form of stock certificate attached hereto as Exhibit C is adopted as the form of certificate of the Common Stock.

8. Qualification to Do Business

RESOLVED: That the Company be qualified to do business in any jurisdiction that the Director(s) may deem from time to time to be necessary to be so qualified and that the officers of the Company be, and they hereby are, authorized and empowered to execute and file, in the name of and on behalf of the Company, with the Secretary of State of such jurisdictions any and all documents, certificates or the like necessary to effect such qualification of the Company as a foreign Company in such jurisdiction.

9. Bank Accounts

RESOLVED: That the Chief Financial Officer, or any other officer of the Corporation, as deemed appropriate by the Director(s) of the Company, and each of them acting singly hereby is, authorized and directed, in the name and on behalf of the Company, to open such accounts with such banking institution as the officers deem necessary or appropriate to conduct the business of the Company; that the Company hereby adopts, as though the same were presented herewith, any standard form of resolution required by any banking institution in order for the Company to establish an account with such banking institution; and that the officers of the Company be, and hereby are, authorized to certify the adoption of any such resolution and are directed to record any resolutions so certified in the Company's minute book.

10. Employer Identification Number

RESOLVED: That the proper officers of the Company are directed to apply to the IRS district Director for an employer's identification number.

11. Indemnification

RESOLVED: That the Company shall enter into an indemnification Agreement Substantially with each of the Company's present and future directors and officers.

12. Sub Chapter C Election

RESOLVED: That the election to be taxed as a small business corporation under Subchapter C of Chapter 1 of the Internal Revenue Code of 1986 be submitted to the shareholders for their consent, and that upon obtaining said consent, the officers of the corporation shall prepare and submit the necessary documents and forms to accomplish said election.

13. General

RESOLVED: To authorize, empower and direct the officers of the Company, and each of them acting singly (i) to execute, seal and deliver in the name of and on behalf of the Company any and all documents, agreements, and instruments to effectuate any of the foregoing resolutions, all with such changes herein as any of such officers may deem necessary or desirable, and (ii) to take such action (including without limitation the filing of any and all applications and the payment of any and all filing fees and expenses), or to cause the Company or any other person to take such action as may in the judgment of the officer so acting be necessary or desirable in connection with, or in furtherance of, any of the foregoing resolutions, and the execution and delivery of any such document, agreement or instrument or the taking of any such action shall be conclusive evidence of such officer's authority hereunder to so act.

RESOLVED: To ratify, confirm, and approve all actions taken by the officers of the Company in connection with any and all of the transactions referred to in or contemplated by any of the foregoing resolutions.

RESOLVED: To direct that this Consent be filed with the records of meetings of the Directors.

This action of Incorporator shall be filed in the Minute book of the Company and shall be effective as of the date first written above.

ByLaws

RK ENGINEERING WORKS
A California Corporation

Los Angeles, CA 90034

BYLAWS

OF

█████████ WORKS, INC.

A CALIFORNIA CORPORATION

ARTICLE I

OFFICES

SECTION 1. PRINCIPAL EXECUTIVE OFFICE. The principal office of the corporation shall be located at such place as the Board of Directors shall from time to time determine.

SECTION 2. OTHER OFFICES. Other offices may at any time be established by the Board of Directors at any place or places where the corporation is qualified to do business.

ARTICLE II

MEETINGS OF SHAREHOLDERS

SECTION 1. PLACE OF MEETINGS. All meetings of shareholders shall be held at the principal executive office of the corporation or at any other place which may be designated either by the board of Directors or by the Shareholders in accordance with these bylaws.

SECTION 2. ANNUAL MEETINGS. The annual meetings of shareholders shall be held on such date and time as shall be designated from time to time by the Board of Directors or by the Shareholders in accordance with these Bylaws. If the date set forth in these Bylaws falls upon a legal holiday, then such annual meeting of shareholders shall be held at the same time and place on the next day thereafter ensuing which is not a legal holiday. At such annual meetings, Directors shall be elected, and any other business may be transacted which is within the powers of the Shareholders.

SECTION 3. SPECIAL MEETINGS. Special meetings of the Shareholders, for the purpose of taking any action which is within the powers of the Shareholders, may be called at any time by the Chairman of the Board or the President or by the Board of Directors, or by the holders of shares entitled to cast not less than ten percent of the votes at the meeting. Upon request in writing that a special meeting of Shareholders be called for any proper purpose, directed to the Chairman of the Board, President, Vice President or Secretary by any person (other than the board) entitled to call a special meeting of Shareholders, the officer forthwith shall cause notice to be given to the Shareholders entitled to vote that a meeting will be held at a time requested by the person or persons calling the meeting, not less than thirty nor more than sixty days after receipt of request.

SECTION 4. NOTICE OF MEETINGS OF SHAREHOLDERS. Written notice of each meeting of Shareholders, whether annual or special, shall be given to each shareholder entitled to vote thereat, either personally or by mail or other means of written communication, charges prepaid, addressed to such Shareholder at the address of such Shareholder appearing on the books of the corporation or given by such Shareholder to the Corporation for the purpose of notice. If any notice addressed to the Shareholder at the address of such Shareholder appearing on the books of the corporation is returned to the Corporation by the United States Postal Service marked to indicate that the United States Postal Service is unable to deliver the notice to the Shareholder at such address, all future notices shall be deemed to have been duly given without further mailing if the same shall be available for the Shareholder upon written demand of the Shareholder at the principal executive office of the Corporation for a period of one year from the date of the giving the notice to other Shareholders. If no address appears on the books of the Corporation or is given by the Shareholder to the Corporation for the purpose of notice, notice shall be deemed to have been given to such Shareholder or sent by mail or other means of written communication addressed to the place where the principal executive office of the corporation is located, or if published at least once in a newspaper of general circulation in the county in which the principal executive office is located.

(a) Without limiting the manner by which notice otherwise may be given effectively to Shareholders, any notice to Shareholders given by the Corporation shall be effective if given by a form of electronic submission consented to by the Shareholder to whom the notice is given. Any such consent shall be revocable by the Shareholder by written notice to the Corporation. Any such consent shall be revocable by the Shareholder by written notice to the Corporation. Any such consent shall be deemed revoked of (i) the Corporation is unable to deliver by electronic transmission (2) consecutive notices given by the Corporation in accordance with such consent and (ii) such inability becomes known to the Secretary or an Assistant Secretary of the Corporation or to the transfer agent, or other person responsible for the giving of notice; provided, however, the inadvertent failure to treat such inability as a revocation shall not invalidate any meeting or other action.

(b) Notice given pursuant to subsection (a) of this Section shall be deemed given: (1) if by facsimile telecommunication, when directed to a number at which the Shareholder has consented to receive notice, (2) of by electronic mail, when directed to an electronic mail address at which the Shareholder has consented to receive notice; (3) if by a posting on an electronic network together with separate notice to the Shareholder of such specific posting, upon the later of (A) such posting and (B) the giving of such separate notice; and (4) if by any other form of electronic transmission, when directed to the Shareholder.

(c) For purposes of this Section, "electronic transmission" means any form of communication, not directly involving the physical transmission of paper, that creates a record that may be retained, retrieved, and reviewed by a recipient thereof, and that may be directly reproduced in paper form by such a recipient through an automated process.

All such notices shall be given to each Shareholder entitled thereto not less than ten days nor more than sixty days before the meeting. Any such notice shall be deemed to have been given at the time when delivered personally or deposited in the mail or sent by other means of written communication. An affidavit of mailing of any such notice in accordance with the foregoing provisions, executed by the Secretary, Assistant Secretary or any transfer agent of the Corporation shall be prima facia evidence of the giving of notice.

All such notices shall state the place, date and hour of such meeting. In the case of a special meeting such notice shall also state the general nature of the business to be transacted at such meeting, and no other business may be transacted thereat. In the case of an annual meeting, such notice shall also state those matters which the Board of Directors at the time of the mailing of the notice intends to present for action by the Shareholders. Any proper matter may be presented at an annual meeting of Shareholders through not stated in the notice, provided that unless the general nature of a proposal to be approved by the Shareholders relating to the following matters is stated in the notice or a written waiver of notice, any such Shareholder approval will require unanimous approval of all Shareholders entitled to vote:

i. A proposal to approve or other transaction between the corporation and one or more of its Directors or any corporation, firm or association in which one or more of its Directors has a material financial interest or is also a Director;
ii. A proposal to amend the Articles of Incorporation;
iii. A proposal to approve the principal terms of a reorganization as defined in Section 181 of the General Corporation Law;
iv. A proposal to wind up and dissolve the corporation; and/or

The notice of any meeting at which Directors are to be elected shall include the names of nominees intended at the time of the notice to be presented by management for election.

SECTION 5. QUORUM. The presence in person or by proxy of the holders of a majority of the shares entitled to vote any meeting shall constitute a quorum for the transaction of business. The Shareholders present at a duly called or held meeting at which a quorum is present may continue to transact business until adjournment, nor withstanding the withdrawal of enough Shareholders to leave less than a quorum, if any action taken (other than adjournment) is approved by at least a majority of the shares required to constitute a quorum.

SECTION 6. ADJOURNED MEETINGS AND NOTICE THEREOF. Any Shareholder's meeting, annual or special, whether or not a quorum is present, may be adjourned from time to time by vote of a majority of the shares of the holders of which are either present in person or by proxy threat, but in the absence of a quorum, no other business may be transacted at any such meeting, except as provided in Section 4 of this Article.

When any Shareholder's meeting, either annual or special, is adjourned for forty-five (45) days or more, or if after the adjournment a new record date is fixed for the adjourned meeting, notice of the adjourned meeting shall be given to each Shareholder of record entitled to vote at the adjourned meeting as in the case of an original meeting. Except as set forth in this Section 6 or Article II, it shall not be necessary to give any notice of an adjourned meeting or of the business to be transacted at an adjourned meeting, other than by announcement of the time and place thereof at the meeting at which such adjournment is taken.

SECTION 7. VOTING. At all meetings of Shareholders, every Shareholder entitled to vote shall have the right to vote in person or by proxy the number of shares standing in the name of such shareholder on the stock records of the corporation on the record date for such meeting. Shares held by an administrator, executor, guardian, conservator, custodian, trustee, receiver, pledge, minor, corporation or fiduciary or held by this corporation or a subsidiary of this corporation in a fiduciary capacity or by two or more persons shall be voted in the manner set forth in Sections 702, 703 and 704 of the General Corporation Law. Shares of this corporation owned by this corporation or a subsidiary (except shares held in a fiduciary capacity) shall not be entitled to vote. Unless a record date for voting purposes is fixed pursuant to Section 1 of Article V of these Bylaws, then only persons in whose names shares entitled to vote stand on the stock records of the corporation at the close of business day next preceding the day on which notice is given or, of notice is waiver, at the close of business on the business day next preceding the day on which the meeting is held, shall be entitled to vote at such meeting, and such day shall be record date for such meeting. Votes at a meeting may be given by via voce or by ballot; provided, however, that all elections for Directors must be by ballot upon demand made by a Shareholder at any election and before the voting begins. If a quorum is present at the beginning of the meeting, except with respect to the election of Directors (and subject to provisions of Section 5 of this Article II should Shareholders withdraw thereafter) the affirmative vote of the majority of the shares represented at the meeting and entitled to vote on any matter shall be the act of the Shareholders and shall decide any question properly brought before the meeting, unless the vote of a greater number or voting by classes is required shall govern and control and decision of such question. Subject to the provisions of the next sentence, at all elections of Directors of the corporation, each Shareholder shall be entitled to cumulate his votes unless the name of the candidate or candidates for whom such votes would be cast has been placed in nomination prior to the voting and any Shareholder has given notice at the meeting prior to the voting, of such Shareholder's intention to cumulate his votes. The candidates receiving the highest number of votes up to the number of Directors to be elected shall be elected.

SECTION 8. WAIVER OF NOTICE AND CONSENT OF ABSENTEES. The proceedings and transactions of any meeting of Shareholders, either annual or special, however called and noticed and whether held, shall be as valid as though had at a meeting duly held after regular call and notice, if a quorum is present either in person or by proxy, and if, either before or after the meeting, each of the persons entitled to vote, not present in person or proxy, signs a written waiver of notice or a consent to the holding of such meeting, or an approval of the minutes thereof. Attendance of a person at a meeting shall constitute a waiver of notice of such meeting, except when the person objects, at the beginning, to the transaction of any business because the meeting is not lawfully called or convened and except that attendance at a meeting is not a waiver of any right to object to the consideration of matters required by law or these Bylaws to be included in the notice but which was not so included, if such objection at the beginning of the meeting or to the consideration of matters required to be but not included in the notice may orally withdraw such objection at the meeting or thereafter waive such objection by signing a written waiver thereof or a consent to the holding of the meeting or the consideration of the matter or an approval of the minutes of the meeting. Neither the business to be transacted at nor the purpose of any annual or special meeting of Shareholders need be specified in any written waiver of notice except that the general nature of the proposals specified in subsections (a) through (e) of Section 4 this Article II, shall be so stated. All such waivers, consents or approvals shall be filed with the corporate records or made a part of the minutes of the meeting.

SECTION 9. ACTION WITHOUT MEETING. Directors may be elected without a meeting by a consent in writing, setting forth the action so taken, signed by all of the persons who would be entitled to vote for the election of Directors, provided that, without notice except as hereinafter set forth, a

Director may be elected at any time to fill a vacancy not filled by the Directors by the written consent of persons holding a majority of the outstanding shares entitled to vote for the election of Directors.

Any other action which, under any provision of the General Corporation Law may be taken at any annual or special meeting of the Shareholders, may be taken without a meeting, and without notice except as hereinafter set forth, if a consent in writing, setting forth the action so taken, is signed by the holders of outstanding shares having not less than the minimum number of votes that would be necessary to authorize or take such action at a meeting at which all shares entitled to vote thereon were present and voted. Unless the consents of all Shareholders entitled to vote have been solicited in writing:

(i) Notice of any proposed Shareholder approval of (i) a contract or other transaction between the corporation and one or more of its Directors or any corporation and one or more of its Directors or any corporation, firm or association in which one or more of its Directors has a material financial interest or is also a Director, (ii) indemnification of an agent of the corporation as authorized by Section 16, of Article III, of these Bylaws, (iii) a reorganization of the corporation as defined in Section 181 of the General Corporation Law, or (iv) the distribution of shares, obligations or securities of any other corporation or assets other than money which is not in accordance with the liquidation rights of preferred shares if the corporation is in the process of winding up, without a meeting by less than unanimous written consent, shall be given at least ten (10) days before the consummation of the action authorized by such approval; and

(ii) Prompt notice shall be given of the taking of any other corporate action approved by Shareholders without a meeting by less than unanimous written consent, to those Shareholders entitled to vote who have not consented in writing. Such notices shall be given in the manner and shall be deemed to have been given as provided in Section 4 of Article II of these Bylaws.

Unless, as provided in Section 1 of Article V of these bylaws, the Board of Directors has fixed a record date for the determination of Shareholders entitled to notice of and to give such written consent, the record date for such determination shall be the day on which the first written consent is give. All such written consents shall be filed with the Secretary of the Corporation.

Any Shareholder giving a written consent, or the Shareholder's proxyholders, or a transferee of the shares or a personal representative of the Shareholder or their respective proxyholders, may revoke the consent by a writing received by the corporation prior to the time that written consents of the number of shares required to authorize the proposed action have been filed with the Secretary of the corporation, but may not do so thereafter. Such revocation is effective upon its receipt by the Secretary of the corporation.

SECTION 10. PROXIES. Every person entitled to vote or execute consents shall have the right to do so either in person or by an agent or agents authorized by a written proxy executed by such person or the duly authorized agent of such person and filed with the Secretary of the corporation, or the persons appointed as inspectors of election or such other person as may be designated by the Board of Directors or the Chief Executive Officer to receive proxies; provided, that no such proxy shall be valid after the expiration of eleven months from the date of its execution, unless the Shareholder executing it specifies therein the length of time for which such proxy is to continue in force. Every proxy duly executed continues in full force and effect until revoked by the person executing it prior to the vote pursuant thereto. Except as otherwise provided by law, such revocation may be effected by attendance at the meeting and voting in person by the person executing the proxy or by a writing stating that the proxy is revoked or by a proxy bearing a later date executed by the person executing the proxy and filed with the Secretary of the corporation or the persons appointed as inspectors of election or such other persons as may be designated by the Board of Directors or the Chief Executive Officer to receive proxies.

SECTION 11. INSPECTORS OF ELECTION. In advance of any meeting of Shareholders, the Board of Directors may appoint any persons as inspectors of election to act at such meeting or any adjournment thereof. If inspectors of election are not so appointed, or if any persons so appointed fail to appear or refuse to act, the Chairman of any such meeting may, and on the request of any Shareholder or his proxy shall, make such appointment at the meeting. The number of inspectors shall be either one or three. If appointed at a meeting on the request of one or more Shareholders or proxies, the majority of shares represented in person or by proxy shall determine whether one or three inspectors are to be appointed.

The inspectors of election shall determine the number of shares outstanding and the voting power of each, the shares represented at the meeting, the existence of a quorum and the authenticity, validity and effect of proxies, receive votes, ballots or consents, hear and determine all challenges and questions in any way arising in connection with the right to vote, count and tabulate all votes or consents, determine when the polls shall close, determine the result and do such acts as may be proper to conduct the election or vote with fairness to all Shareholders. In the determination of the validity and effect of proxies the dates contained on the forms of proxy shall presumptively determine the order of execution of the proxies, regardless of the postmark dates on the envelopes in which they are mailed.

The inspectors of election shall perform their duties impartially, in good faith, to the best of their ability and as expeditiously as is practical. If there are three inspectors of election, the decision, act or certificate of a majority is effective in all respects as the decision, act or certificate of all. Any report or certificate made by the inspectors of election is prima facie evidence of the facts stated therein.

ARTICLE III

DIRECTORS

SECTION 1. POWERS. Subject to the General Corporation Law and any limitations in the Articles of Incorporation relating to action requiring Shareholder approval, and subject to the duties of Directors as prescribed by the Bylaws, the business and affairs of the corporation shall be managed and all corporate powers shall be exercised by or under the direction of the Board of Directors.

SECTION 2. NUMBER OF DIRECTORS. The authorized number of Directors shall be as fixed by the Shareholders, and shall remain so until changed by a duly adopted amendment to the Articles of Incorporation or by an amendment to these Bylaws adopted by the vote or written consent of holders of a majority of the outstanding shares then entitled to vote, as provided in Section 212 of the Corporations Code of California; provided, however, that so long as the Corporation has only one shareholder, there may be only one (1) Director. As of the date of adoption of these Bylaws, the Shareholders have fixed the number of Board members at three (3).

SECTION 3. ELECTION AND TERM OF OFFICE. Directors shall be elected at each annual meeting of Shareholders, but if any such annual meeting is not held or the Directors are not elected at any annual meeting, the Directors may be elected at any special meeting of Shareholders held for that purpose, or at the next annual meeting of Shareholders held thereafter. Each Director shall hold office at the pleasure of the Shareholders until the next annual meeting of Shareholders and until his successor has been elected and qualified or until his earlier resignation or removal or his office has been declared vacant in the manner provided in these Bylaws.

SECTION 4. RESIGNATION AND REMOVAL OF DIRECTORS. Any Director may resign effective upon giving written notice to the Board, unless the notice specifies a later time for the effectiveness of such resignation, in which case such resignation shall be effective at the time specified. Unless such resignation specifies otherwise, its acceptance by the corporation shall not be necessary to make it effective. The Board of Directors may declare vacant the office of a Director who has been declared of unsound mind by an order of court or convicted of a felony. Any or all of the Directors may be removed without cause if such removal is approved by the affirmative vote of a majority of the outstanding shares entitled to vote provided that no Director may be removed (unless the entire Board is removed) when the votes cast against removal (or, if such action is taken by written consent, the shares held by persons not consenting in writing to such removal) would be sufficient to elect such Director if voted cumulatively at an election at which the same total number of votes were cast (or, if such action is taken by written consent, all shares entitled to vote were voted) and the entire number of Directors authorized at the time of the Director's most recent election were then being elected. No reduction of the authorized number of Directors shall have the effect of removing any Director before his term of office expires.

SECTION 5. VACANCIES. Vacancies on the Board of Directors (except vacancies created by the removal of a Director) may be filled by a majority of the Directors then in office, whether or not less than a quorum, or by a sole remaining Director, and each Director elected in this manner shall hold office until the next annual meeting of Shareholders and until a successor has been elected and qualified or until his earlier resignation or removal or his office has been declared vacant in the manner provided in these Bylaws. A vacancy or vacancies on the Board of Directors shall exist on the death, resignation or removal of any Director, or if the Board declares vacant the office of a Director if he is declared of unsound mind by an order of court or is convicted of a felony, or if the authorized number of Directors is increased, or if the Shareholders fail to elect the full authorized number of Directors to be voted for at any Shareholders meeting at which an election of Directors is held. The Shareholders may elect a Director at any time to fill any vacancy not filled by the Directors or which occurs by reason of the removal of a Director. Any such election by written consent of Shareholders shall require the consent of a majority of the outstanding shares entitled to vote, except that any such election by written consent of Shareholders to fill any vacancy which occurs by reason of the removal of a Director shall require the unanimous consent of the outstanding shares entitled to vote. If the resignation of a Director states that it is to be effective at a future time, a successor may be elected to take office when the resignation becomes effective.

SECTION 6. PLACE OF MEETINGS. Regular and special meetings of the Board of Directors shall be held at any place within or without the State of California which has been designated in the notice or written waiver of notice of the meeting, or, if not stated in the notice or waiver of notice or there is no notice, designated by resolution of the Board of Directors or, either before or after the meeting, consented to in writing by all members of the Board who were not present at the meeting. If the place of a regular or special meeting is not designated in the notice or waiver of notice or fixed by a resolution of the Board or consented to in writing by all members of the Board not present at the meeting, it shall be held at the corporation's principal executive office.

SECTION 7. REGULAR MEETINGS. Immediately following each annual Shareholders' meeting, the Board of Directors shall hold a regular meeting to elect officers and transact other business. Such meeting shall be held at the same place as the annual meeting or such other place as shall be fixed by the Board of Directors. Other regular meetings of the Board of Directors shall be held at such times and places as fixed by the Board. Call and notice of regular meetings of the Board of Directors shall not be required and is hereby dispensed with.

SECTION 8. SPECIAL MEETINGS. Special meetings of the Board of Directors for any purpose or purposes may be called at any time by the Chairman of the Board, the President, any Vice President, the Secretary, any Assistant Secretary or any two Directors. Notice of the time and place of special meetings shall be delivered personally or by telephone (including a voice messaging system or other system or technology designed to record and communicate messages), telegraph, facsimile, electronic mail or other electronic means, or sent to the Director by mail. In case notice is given by mail or telegram, it shall be sent, charges prepaid, addressed to the Director at his address appearing on the corporate records, or if it is not on these records or is not readily ascertainable, at the place where the meetings of the Directors are regularly held. If notice is given by mail, it shall be deposited in the United States mail at least four (4) days before the meeting. If notice is given by telegraph, facsimile, electronic mail or other electronic means, it shall be personally delivered to the recipient, or delivered to a common carrier for transmission to the recipient, or actually transmitted by the person giving the notice by electronic means to the recipient, at least forty-eight (48) hours before the meeting. If notice is given in person or by telephone (including a voice messaging system or other system or technology designed to record and communicate messages), it shall be given to the recipient (including the recipient's designated voice mailbox or address on such a system), or to a person at the office of the recipient who the person giving notice has reason to believe will promptly communicate it to the recipient, at least forty-eight (48) hours before the meeting. Such forms of communication, as provided in this Section, shall be due, legal and personal notice to such Director.

SECTION 9. QUORUM. A majority of the authorized number of Directors shall constitute a quorum of the Board for the transaction of business, except to adjourn a meeting under Section 11. Every act or decision done or made by a majority of the Directors present at a meeting duly held at which a quorum is present is the act of the Board of Directors, unless the vote of a greater number or the same number after disqualifying one or more Directors from voting, is required by law, the Articles of Incorporation or these Bylaws. A meeting at which a quorum is initially present may continue to transact business notwithstanding the withdrawal of Directors, provided that any action taken is approved by at least a majority of the required quorum for such meeting.

SECTION 10. WAIVER OF NOTICE OR CONSENT. The transactions of any meeting of the Board of Directors, however called and noticed or wherever held, shall be as valid as though had at a meeting duly held after regular call and notice, if a quorum is present and if, either before or after the meeting, each of the Directors not present or who, though present, has prior to the meeting or at its commencement, protested the lack of proper notice to him, signs a written waiver of notice, or a consent to holding the meeting, or an approval of the minutes of the meeting. All such waivers, consents and approvals shall be filed with the corporate records or made a part of the minutes of the meeting. A notice or waiver of notice need not specify the purpose of any regular or special meeting of the Board of Directors. Notice of a meeting need not be given to any Director who signs a waiver of notice, whether before or after the meeting, or who attends the meeting without protesting, prior to or at its commencement, the lack of notice to such Director.

SECTION 11. ADJOURNMENT. A majority of the Directors present, whether or not a quorum is present, may adjourn any meeting to another time and place. If the meeting is adjourned for more than 24 hours, notice of the adjournment to another time or place shall be given prior to the time of the adjourned meeting to the Directors who were not present at the time of the adjournment.

SECTION 12. MEETINGS BY CONFERENCE TELEPHONE, ELECTRONIC VIDEO SCREEN EQUIPMENT, ETC. Members of the Board of Directors may participate in a meeting through use of conference telephone, electronic video screen communication or other communications equipment. Participation in a meeting through use of conference telephone pursuant to this Section constitutes presence in person at that meeting as long as all members participating in the meeting are able to hear one another. Participation in a meeting through the use of electronic video screen communication or other communications equipment (other than conference telephone) pursuant to this Section constitutes presence in person at that meeting if all of the following apply: (a) each member participating in the meeting can communicate with all of the other members concurrently; (b) each member is provided with the means of participating in all matters before the Board of Directors, including, without limitation, the capacity to propose, or to interpose an objection to, a specific action to be taken by the corporation; and (c) the corporation adopts and implements some means of verifying both of the following: (1) that a person participating in the meeting is a Director, or other person entitled to participate in such meeting and (2) that all actions of, or votes by, the Board are taken or cast only by the Directors and not by persons who are not Directors.

SECTION 13. ACTION WITHOUT A MEETING. Any action required or permitted to be taken by the Board of Directors may be taken without a meeting, if all members of the Board shall individually or collectively consent in writing to such action. Such written consent or consents shall be filed with the minutes of the proceedings of the Board. Such action by written consent shall have the same force and effect as a unanimous vote of such Directors.

SECTION 14. FEES AND COMPENSATION. Unless otherwise determined by the Board by resolution, Directors and members of committees shall receive neither financial compensation for their services as Directors or members of committees nor reimbursement for their expenses incurred as Directors or members of committees. Directors and members of committees may receive compensation and reimbursement for their expenses incurred as officers, agents or employees of or for other services performed for the corporation as approved by the Chief Executive Officer without authorization, approval or ratification by the Board.

SECTION 15. COMMITTEES. The Board of Directors may, at its discretion, by resolution adopted by a majority of the authorized number of Directors, designate one or more committees, each of which shall be composed of two or more Directors, to serve at the pleasure of the Board. The Board may designate one or more Directors as alternate members of any committee, who may replace any absent member at any meeting of the committee. The Board may delegate to any such committee, to the extent provided in such resolution, any of the Board's powers and authority in the management of the corporation's business and affairs, except with respect to:

(i) The approval of any action for which the General Corporation Law or the Articles of Incorporation also requires approval by the Shareholders;

(ii) The filling of vacancies on the Board of Directors or any committee;

(iii) The fixing of compensation of Directors for serving on the Board or on any committee;

(iv) The amendment or repeal of Bylaws or the adoption of new Bylaws;

(v) The amendment or repeal of any resolution of the Board which by its express terms is not so amendable or repealable;

(vi) a distribution to the Shareholders of the corporation, except at a rate or in a periodic amount or within a price range determined by the Board; and

(vii) the appointment of other committees of the Board or the members thereof.

The Board may prescribe appropriate rules, not inconsistent with these Bylaws, by which proceedings of any such committee shall be conducted. The provisions of these Bylaws relating to the calling of meetings of the Board, notice of meetings of the Board and waiver of such notice, adjournments of meetings of the Board, written consents to Board meetings and approval of minutes, action by the Board by consent in writing without a meeting, the place of holding such meetings, meetings by conference telephone or similar communications equipment, the quorum for such meetings, the vote required at such meetings and the withdrawal of Directors after commencement of a meeting shall apply to committees of the Board and action by such committees. In addition, any member of the committee designated by the Board as the Chairman or as Secretary of the committee or any two members of a committee may call meetings of the committee. Regular meetings of any committee may be held without notice if the time and place of such meetings are fixed by the Board of Directors or the committee.

SECTION 16. INDEMNIFICATION OF CORPORATE AGENTS.

(i) For the purposes of this section, "agent" means any person who is or was a Director, officer, employee or other agent of this corporation, or is or was serving at the request of this corporation as a Director, officer, employee or agent of another foreign or domestic corporation, partnership, joint venture, trust or other enterprise, or was a Director, officer, employee or agent of a foreign or domestic corporation which was a predecessor corporation of this corporation or of another enterprise at the request of such predecessor corporation; "proceeding" means any threatened, pending or completed action or proceeding, whether civil, criminal, administrative or investigative; and "expenses" includes without limitation, attorneys' fees and any expenses of establishing a right to indemnification under subdivision (d) or paragraph (3) of subdivision (e).

(ii) This corporation shall have the power to indemnify any person who was or is a party or is threatened to be made a party to any proceeding (other than an action by or in the right of this corporation to procure a judgment in its favor) by reason of the fact that such person is or was an agent of this corporation, against expenses, judgments, fines, settlements and other amounts actually and reasonably incurred in connection with such proceeding if such person acted in good faith and in a manner such person reasonably believed to be in the best interests of this corporation and, in the case of a criminal proceeding, had no reasonable cause to believe the conduct of such person was unlawful. The termination of any proceeding by judgment, order, settlement, conviction or upon a plea of nolo contendere or its equivalent shall not, of itself, create a presumption that the person did not act in good faith and in a manner which the person reasonably believed to be in the best interests of this corporation or that the person had reasonable cause to believe that the person's conduct was unlawful

(iii) This corporation shall have the power to indemnify any person who was or is a party, or is threatened to be made a party, to any threatened, pending or completed action by or in the right of this corporation to procure a judgment in its favor by reason of the fact that such person is or was an agent of this corporation, against expenses actually and reasonably incurred by such person in connection with the defense or settlement of such action if such person acted in good faith, in a manner such person believed to be in the best interests of this corporation and its Shareholders.

No indemnification shall be made under this subdivision for any of the following:

(1) in respect of any claim, issue or matter as to which such person shall have been adjudged to be liable to this corporation in the performance of such person's duty to this corporation and its Shareholders, unless and only to the extent that the court in which such proceeding is or was pending shall determine upon application that, in view of all the circumstances of the case, such person is fairly and reasonably entitled to indemnity for the expenses and then only to the extent that the court shall determine.

(2) Of amounts paid in settling or otherwise disposing of a pending action without court approval.

(3) Of expenses incurred in defending a pending action which is settled or otherwise disposed of without court approval.

(iv) To the extent that an agent of this corporation has been successful on the merits in defense of any proceeding referred to in subdivision (b) or (c) or in defense of any claim, issue or matter therein, the agent shall be indemnified against expenses actually and reasonably incurred by the agent in connection therewith.

(v) Except as provided in subdivision (d), any indemnification under this Section shall be made by this corporation only if authorized in the specific case, upon a determination that indemnification of the agent is proper in the circumstances because the agent has met the applicable standard of conduct set forth in subdivision (b) or (c), by any of the following:

(1) A majority vote of a quorum consisting of Directors who are not parties to such proceeding.

(2) If such a quorum of Directors is not obtainable, by independent legal counsel in a written opinion.

(3) Approval of the Shareholders (Section 153 of the California Corporations Code) with the shares owned by the person to be indemnified not being entitled to vote thereon.

(4) The court in which such proceeding is or was pending upon application made by this corporation or the agent or the attorney or other person rendering services in connection with the defense, whether or not such application by the agent, attorney or other person is opposed by this corporation.

(vi) Expenses incurred in defending any proceeding may be advanced by this corporation prior to the final disposition of such proceeding upon receipt of an undertaking by or on behalf of the agent to repay such amount if it shall be determined ultimately that the agent is not entitled to be indemnified as authorized in this Section. The provisions of subdivision (a) of Section 315 of the General Corporation Law do not apply to advances made pursuant to this subdivision.

(vii) The indemnification provided by this section shall not be deemed exclusive of any other rights to which those seeking indemnification may be entitled under any bylaw, agreement, vote of Shareholders or disinterested Directors or otherwise, both as to action in an official capacity and as to action in another capacity while holding such office, to the extent that such additional rights to indemnification are authorized in the Articles of Incorporation of this corporation. The rights to indemnity hereunder shall continue as to a person who has ceased to be a Director, officer, employee, or agent and shall inure to the benefit of the heirs, executors and administrators of the person. Nothing contained in this Section shall affect any right to indemnification to which persons other than such Directors and officers of this corporation may be entitled by contract or otherwise.

(viii) No indemnification or advance shall be made under this Section, except as provided in subdivision (d) or paragraph (3) of subdivision (e), in any circumstance where it appears:

(1) That it would be inconsistent with a provision of the Articles of Incorporation, Bylaws, a resolution of the Shareholders or an agreement in effect at the time of the accrual of the alleged cause of action asserted in the proceeding in which the expenses were incurred or other amounts were paid, which prohibits or otherwise limits indemnification.

(2) That it would be inconsistent with any condition expressly imposed by a court in approving a settlement.

(ix) This corporation shall have the power to purchase and maintain insurance on behalf of any agent of the corporation against any liability asserted against or incurred by the agent in such capacity or arising out of the agent's status as such whether or not this corporation would have the power to indemnify the agent against such liability under the provisions of this section. The fact that a corporation owns all or a portion of the shares of the company issuing a policy of insurance shall not render this subdivision inapplicable if either of the following conditions are satisfied: (1) If authorized in the Articles of Incorporation of the corporation, any policy issued is limited to the extent provided by subdivision (d) of Section 204 of the California Corporations Code; or (2) (A) the company issuing the insurance policy is organized, licensed, and operated in a manner that complies with the insurance laws and regulations applicable to its jurisdiction of organization, (B) the company issuing the policy provides procedures for processing claims that do not permit that company to be subject to the direct control of the corporation that purchased that policy, and (C) the policy issued provides for some manner of risk sharing between the issuer and purchaser of the policy, on one hand, and some unaffiliated person or persons, on the other, such as by providing for more than one unaffiliated owner of the company issuing the policy or by providing that a portion of the coverage furnished will be obtained from some unaffiliated insurer or reinsurer.

ARTICLE IV.

OFFICERS

SECTION 1. OFFICERS AND OTHERS. The officers of the corporation shall be a Chief Executive Officer or a President, or both, a Secretary and a Chief Financial Officer. The corporation may also have, at the discretion of the Board of Directors, one or more Vice Presidents, one or more Assistant Secretaries, one or more Assistant Treasurers and such other officers as may be appointed in accordance with the provisions of Section 3 of this Article. Any two (2) or more offices may be held by the same person.

SECTION 2. ELECTIONS. The officers of the corporation, except such officers as may be appointed in accordance with the provisions of Section 3 or Section 5 of this Article, shall be chosen annually by the Board of Directors, and each such officer shall serve at the pleasure of the Board of Directors until the regular meeting of the Board of Directors following the annual meeting of Shareholders and until his successor is elected and qualified or until his earlier resignation or removal.

SECTION 3. OTHER OFFICERS. The Board of Directors may appoint, and may empower the Chairman of the Board or the President or both of them to appoint, such other officers as the business of the corporation may require, each of whom shall hold office for such period, have such authority and perform such duties as are provided in the Bylaws or as the Board of Directors may from time to time determine.

SECTION 4. REMOVAL AND RESIGNATION. Any officer may be removed with or without cause either by the Board of Directors or, except for an officer chosen by the Board, by any officer upon whom the power of removal may be conferred by the Board (subject, in each case, to the rights, if any, of an officer under any contract of employment). Any officer may resign at any time upon written notice to the corporation (without prejudice however, to the rights, if any, of the corporation under any contract to which the officer is a party). Any such resignation shall take effect upon receipt of such notice or at any later time specified therein. If the resignation is effective at a future time, a successor may be elected to take office when the resignation becomes effective. Unless a resignation specifies otherwise, its acceptance by the corporation shall not be necessary to make it effective.

SECTION 5. VACANCIES. A vacancy in any office because of death, resignation, removal, disqualification or any other cause shall be filled in a manner prescribed in the Bylaws for regular appointments to the office.

SECTION 6. CHAIRMAN OF THE BOARD. The Board of Directors may, in its discretion, elect a Chairman of the Board, who, unless otherwise determined by the Board of Directors, shall preside at all meetings of the Board of Directors at which he is present and shall exercise and perform any other powers and duties assigned to him by the Board or prescribed by the Bylaws. If the office of President is vacant, the Chairman of the Board shall be the general manager and Chief Executive Officer of the corporation and shall exercise the duties of the President as set forth in Section 7.

SECTION 7. PRESIDENT. Subject to any supervisory powers, if any, that may be given by the Board of Directors or the Bylaws to the Chairman of the Board, if there be such an officer, the President shall be the corporation's general manager and Chief Executive Officer and shall, subject to the control of the Board of Directors, have general supervision, direction and control of the business, affairs and officers of the corporation. Unless otherwise determined by the Board of Directors, he shall preside as Chairman at all meetings of the Shareholders, and in the absence of the Chairman of the Board, or if there be none, at all meetings of the Board of Directors. He shall have the general powers and duties of management usually vested in the office of President of a corporation; shall have any other powers and duties that are prescribed by the Board of Directors or the Bylaws; and shall be primarily responsible for carrying out all orders and resolutions of the Board of Directors.

SECTION 8. VICE PRESIDENTS. In the absence or disability of the Chief Executive Officer, the Vice Presidents in order of their rank as fixed by the Board of Directors, or if not ranked, the Vice President designated by the Board of Directors, shall perform all the duties of the Chief Executive Officer, and when so acting, shall have all the powers of, and be subject to all the restrictions on, the Chief Executive Officer. Each Vice President shall have any of the powers and perform any other duties that from time to time may be prescribed for him by the Board of Directors or the Bylaws or the Chief Executive Officer.

SECTION 9. SECRETARY. The Secretary shall keep or cause to be kept a book of minutes of all meetings and actions by written consent of all Directors, Shareholders and committees of the Board of Directors. The minutes of each meeting shall state the time and place that it was held and such other information as shall be necessary to determine whether the meeting was held in accordance with law and these Bylaws and the actions taken thereat. The Secretary shall keep or cause to be kept at the corporation's principal executive office, or at the office of its transfer agent or registrar, a record of the Shareholders of the corporation, giving the names and addresses of all Shareholders and the number and class of shares held by each. The Secretary shall give, or cause to be given, notice of all meetings of Shareholders, Directors and committees required to be given under these Bylaws or by law, shall keep or cause the keeping of the corporate seal in safe custody and shall have any other powers and perform any other duties that are prescribed by the Board of Directors or the Bylaws or the Chief Executive Officer. If the Secretary refuses or fails to give notice of any meeting lawfully called, any other officer of the corporation may give notice of such meeting. The Assistant Secretary, or if there be more than one, any Assistant Secretary, may perform any or all of the duties and exercise any or all of the powers of the Secretary unless prohibited from doing so by the Board of Directors, the Chief Executive Officer or the

Secretary, and shall have such other powers and perform any other duties as are prescribed for him by the Board of Directors or the Chief Executive Officer.

SECTION 10. CHIEF FINANCIAL OFFICER. The Chief Financial Officer shall keep and maintain, or cause to be kept and maintained, adequate and correct books and records of account. The Chief Financial Officer shall cause all money and other valuables in the name and to the credit of the corporation to be deposited at the depositories designated by the Board of Directors or any person authorized by the Board of Directors to designate such depositories. He shall render to the Chief Executive Officer and Board of Directors, when either of them request it, an account of all his transactions as Chief Financial Officer and of the financial condition of the corporation; and shall have any other powers and perform any other duties that are prescribed by the Board of Directors or the Bylaws or the Chief Executive Officer. The Assistant Treasurer, or if there be more than one, any Assistant Treasurer, may perform any or all of the duties and exercise any or all of the powers of the Chief Financial Officer unless prohibited from doing so by the Board of Directors, the Chief Executive Officer or the Chief Financial Officer, and shall have such other powers and perform any other duties as are prescribed for him by the Board of Directors, the Chief Executive Officer or the Chief Financial Officer.

ARTICLE V

MISCELLANEOUS

SECTION 1. RECORD DATE. The Board of Directors may fix a time in the future as a record date for the determination of the Shareholders entitled to notice of and to vote at any meeting of Shareholders or entitled to give consent to corporate action in writing without a meeting, to receive any report, to receive payment of any dividend or other distribution, or allotment of any rights, or to exercise rights with respect to any change, conversion, or exchange of shares or any other lawful action. The record date so fixed shall be not more than sixty days nor less than ten days prior to the date of such meeting, nor more than sixty days prior to any other action for the purposes of which it is fixed. When a record date is so fixed, only Shareholders of record on that date are entitled to notice of and to vote at any such meeting, to give consent without a meeting, to receive any report, to receive a dividend, distribution, or allotment of rights, or to exercise the rights, as the case may be, notwithstanding any transfer of any shares on the books of the corporation after the record date, except as otherwise provided in the Articles of Incorporation or Bylaws.

SECTION 2. INSPECTION OF CORPORATE RECORDS. The books of account, record of Shareholders, and minutes of proceedings of the Shareholders and the Board and committees of the Board of this corporation shall be open to inspection upon the written demand on the corporation of any Shareholder or holder of a voting trust certificate at any time during usual business hours, for a purpose reasonably related to such holder's interests as a Shareholder or as the holder of such voting trust certificate. Such inspection by a Shareholder or holder of a voting trust certificate may be made in person or by agent or attorney, and the right of inspection includes the right to copy and make extracts.

A Shareholder or Shareholders holding at least five percent in the aggregate of the outstanding voting shares of the corporation or who hold at least one percent of such voting shares and have filed a Schedule 14A with the United States Securities and Exchange Commission relating to the election of Directors of the corporation shall have (in person or by agent or attorney) the absolute right to inspect and copy the record of Shareholders' names and addresses and shareholdings during usual business hours upon five business days' prior written demand upon the corporation and to obtain from the transfer agent for the corporation, upon written demand and upon the tender of its usual charges, a list of the Shareholders' names and addresses, who are entitled to vote for the election of Directors, and their shareholdings, as of the most recent record date for which it has been compiled or as of a date specified by the Shareholder subsequent to the date of demand. The list shall be made available on or before the later of five (5) business days after the demand is received or the date specified therein as the date as of which the list is to be compiled.

Every Director shall have the absolute right at any reasonable time to inspect and copy all books, records and documents of every kind and to inspect the physical properties of this corporation and any subsidiary of this corporation. Such inspection by a Director may be made in person or by agent or attorney and the right of inspection includes the right to copy and make extracts.

SECTION 3. CHECKS, DRAFTS, ETC. All checks, drafts or other orders for payment of money, notes or other evidences of indebtedness, issued in the name of or payable to the corporation, shall be signed or endorsed by such person or persons and in such manner as, from time to time, shall be determined by resolution of the Board of Directors. The Board of Directors may authorize one or more officers of the corporation to designate the person or persons authorized to sign such documents and the manner in which such documents shall be signed.

SECTION 4. ANNUAL AND OTHER REPORTS. The statutory requirement that the Board of Directors cause an annual report to be sent to Shareholders is hereby waived.

A Shareholder or Shareholders holding at least five percent (5%) of the outstanding shares of any class of the corporation may make a written request to the corporation for an income statement of the corporation for the three-month, six-month or nine-month period of the current fiscal year ended more than thirty (30) days prior to the date of the request and a balance sheet of the corporation as of the end of such period. In addition, if no annual report for the last fiscal year has been sent to Shareholders, a Shareholder or Shareholders holding at least five percent (5%) of the outstanding shares of any class of the corporation may make a written request to the corporation for an annual report for the last fiscal year, which annual report shall contain a balance sheet as of the end of such fiscal year and an income statement and statement of changes in financial position for such fiscal year, accompanied by any report thereon of independent accountants or, if there is no such report, the certificate of an authorized officer of the corporation that such statements were prepared without audit from the books and records of the corporation. The statements shall be delivered or mailed to the person making the request within thirty days thereafter. A copy of such statements shall be kept on file in the principal executive office of the corporation for twelve months and they shall be exhibited at all reasonable times to any Shareholder demanding an examination of them or a copy shall be mailed to such Shareholder.

The corporation shall, upon the written request of any Shareholder, mail to the Shareholder a copy of the last annual, semiannual or quarterly income statement which it has prepared and a balance sheet as of the end of the period.

The quarterly income statements and balance sheets referred to in this Section shall be accompanied by the report thereon, if any, of any independent accountants engaged by the corporation or the certificate of an authorized officer of the corporation that such financial statements were prepared without audit from the books and records of the corporation.

Unless otherwise determined by the Board of Directors or the Chief Executive Officer, the Chief Financial Officer and any Assistant Treasurer are each authorized officers of the corporation to execute the certificate that the annual report and quarterly income statements and balance sheets referred to in this section were prepared without audit from the books and records of the corporation.

Any report sent to the Shareholders shall be given personally or by mail or other means of written communication, charges prepaid, addressed to such Shareholder at the address of such Shareholder appearing on the books of the corporation or given by such Shareholder to the corporation for the purpose of notice or set forth in the written request of the Shareholder as provided in this Section. If any report addressed to the Shareholder at the address of such Shareholder appearing on the books of the corporation is returned to the corporation by the United States Postal Service marked to indicate that the United States Postal Service is unable to deliver the report to the Shareholder at such address, all future reports shall be deemed to have been duly given without further mailing if the same shall be available for the Shareholder upon written demand of the Shareholder at the principal executive office of the corporation for a period of one year from the date of the giving of the report to all other Shareholders. If no address appears on the books of the corporation or is given by the Shareholder to the corporation for the purpose of notice or is set forth in the written request of the Shareholder as provided in this Section, such report shall be deemed to have been given to such Shareholder if sent by mail or other means of written communication addressed to the place where the principal executive office of the corporation is located, or if published at least once in a newspaper of general circulation in the county in which the principal executive office is located. Any such report shall be deemed to have been given at the time when delivered personally or deposited in the mail or sent by other means of written communication. An affidavit of mailing of any such report in accordance with the foregoing provisions, executed by the Secretary, Assistant Secretary or any transfer agent of the corporation shall be prima facie evidence of the giving of the report.

SECTION 5. CONTRACTS, ETC., HOW EXECUTED. The Board of Directors, except as the Bylaws or Articles of Incorporation otherwise provide, may authorize any officer or officers, agent or agents, to enter into any contract or execute any instrument in the name of and on behalf of the corporation, and such authority may be general or confined to specific instances.

SECTION 6. CERTIFICATE FOR SHARES. Every holder of shares in the corporation shall be entitled to have a certificate or certificates signed in the name of the corporation by the Chairman of the Board or the President or a Vice President and by the Chief Financial Officer or an Assistant Treasurer or the Secretary or any Assistant Secretary, certifying the number of shares and the class or series of shares owned by the Shareholder. Any or all of the signatures on the certificate may be via facsimile. In case any officer, transfer agent or registrar who has signed or whose facsimile signature has been placed upon a certificate shall have ceased to be such officer, transfer agent or registrar before such certificate is issued, it may be issued by the corporation with the same effect as if such person were such officer, transfer agent or registrar at the date of issue.

Any such certificate shall also contain such legend or other statement as may be required by Section 418 of the General Corporation Law, the Corporate Securities Law of 1968, and any agreement between the corporation and the issuee thereof, and may contain such legend or other statement as may be required by any other applicable law or regulation or agreement.

Certificates for shares may be issued prior to full payment thereof, under such restrictions and for such purposes, as the Board of Directors or the Bylaws may provide; provided, however, that any such certificates so issued prior to full payment shall state the total amount of the consideration to be paid therefor and the amount paid thereon.

No new certificate for shares shall be issued in place of any certificate theretofore issued unless the latter is surrendered and cancelled at the same time; provided, however, that a new certificate may be issued without the surrender and cancellation of the old certificate if the certificate theretofore issued is alleged to have been lost, stolen or destroyed. In case of any such allegedly lost, stolen or destroyed certificate, the corporation may require the owner thereof or the legal representative of such owner to give the corporation a bond (or other adequate security) sufficient to indemnify it against any claim that may be made against it (including any expense or liability) on account of the alleged loss, theft or destruction of any such certificate or the issuance of such new certificate.

SECTION 7. REPRESENTATION OF SHARES OF OTHER CORPORATIONS. Unless the Board of Directors shall otherwise determine, the Chairman of the Board, the President, any Vice President, the Secretary and any Assistant Secretary of this corporation are each authorized to vote, represent and exercise on behalf of this corporation all rights incident to any and all shares of any other corporation or corporations standing in the name of this corporation. The authority herein granted to such officers to vote or represent on behalf of this corporation any and all shares held by this corporation in any other corporation or corporations may be exercised either by such officers in person or by any person authorized so to do by proxy or power of attorney or other document duly executed by any such officer.

SECTION 8. STOCK PURCHASE PLAN. The corporation may adopt and carry out a stock purchase plan or agreement or stock option plan or agreement providing for the issue and sale for such consideration as may be fixed of its unissued shares, or of issued shares acquired or to be acquired, to one or more of the employees or directors of the corporation or of a subsidiary or to a trustee on their behalf and for the payment for such shares in installments or at one time, and may provide for aiding any such persons in paying for such shares by compensation for services rendered, promissory notes or otherwise.

Any such stock purchase plan or agreement or stock option plan or agreement may include, among other features, the fixing of eligibility for participation therein, the class and price of shares to be issued or sold under the plan or agreement, the number of shares which may be subscribed for, the method of payment therefor, the reservation of title until full payment therefor, the effect of the termination of employment, option or obligation on the part of the Any such stock purchase plan or agreement or stock option plan or agreement may include, among other features, the fixing of eligibility for participation therein, the class and price of shares to be issued or sold under the plan or agreement, the number of shares which may be subscribed for, the method of payment therefor, the reservation of title until full payment therefor, the effect of the termination of employment, option or obligation on the part of the corporation to repurchase the shares upon termination of employment, restrictions upon transfer of the shares, the time limits of and termination of the plan, and any other matters, not in violation of applicable law, as may be included in the plan as approved or authorized by the Board of Directors or any committee of the Board of Directors.

SECTION 9. INSPECTION OF BYLAWS. The corporation shall keep in its principal executive office in California, or if its principal executive office is not in California, at its principal business office in California, the original or a copy of the Bylaws as amended to date, which shall be open to inspection by the Shareholders at all reasonable times during office hours. If the corporation has no office in

California, it shall upon the written request of any Shareholder, furnish him a copy of the Bylaws as amended to date.

SECTION 10. SEAL. The corporation shall have a common seal, and shall have inscribed thereon the name of the corporation, the date of its incorporation, and the words "INCORPORATED" and "CALIFORNIA".

SECTION 11. CONSTRUCTION AND DEFINITIONS. Unless the context otherwise requires, the general provisions, rules of construction and definitions contained in the General Corporation Law shall govern the construction of these Bylaws. Without limiting the generality of the foregoing, the masculine gender includes the feminine and neuter, the singular number includes the plural and the plural number includes the singular, and the term "Person" includes a corporation as well as a natural person.

ARTICLE VI.

AMENDMENTS

SECTION 1. POWER OF SHAREHOLDERS. New Bylaws may be adopted or these Bylaws may be amended or repealed by the affirmative vote or written consent of a majority of the outstanding shares then entitled to vote, unless otherwise provided by law or the Articles of Incorporation.

SECTION 2. POWER OF DIRECTORS. Subject to the right of Shareholders as provided in Section 1 of this Article VI to adopt, amend or repeal Bylaws, Bylaws other than a bylaw or amendment thereof changing the authorized number of Directors may be adopted, amended or repealed by the Board of Directors.

Adopted by

Stock Issuance/Transfer Ledger and Stock Certificates

RK ENGINEERING WORKS
A California Corporation
███ Rose Avenue #8
Los Angeles CA 90034

Stock Issuance/Transfer Ledger-2014

Name of Stockholder	Place of Residence	Cert. #	No. of shares	Date Issued	Party Shares Transferred from (if original issue, enter as such)	Amount paid thereon	Share Transfer Date	Shares Transferred to	Certificates Surrendered	Number of Shares Held
███	47 Elizabeth Street Artarmon NSW 2064 Australia	CS-001	1	Sep 1, 2014	Original	$10,000.00				
███	47 Elizabeth Street Artarmon NSW 2064 Australia	CS-002	1	Sep 1, 2014	Original	$10,000.00				
███	47 Elizabeth Street Artarmon NSW 2064 Australia	CS-003	1	Sep 1, 2014	Original	$10,000.00				
███	47 Elizabeth Street Artarmon NSW 2064 Australia	CS-004	1	Sep 1, 2014	Original	$10,000.00				
███	47 Elizabeth Street Artarmon NSW 2064 Australia	CS-005	1	Sep 1, 2014	Original	$10,000.00				

№ CS-005   Shares 2

RK ENGINEERING WORKS, INC.

This Certifies that ▮▮▮ is the registered holder of _2_ Shares of the Capital Stock transferable only on the books of the Corporation by the holder hereof in person or by Attorney upon surrender of this Certificate properly endorsed.

In Witness Whereof, the said Corporation has caused this Certificate to be signed by its duly authorized officers and its Corporate Seal is to be hereunto affixed this _01_ day of _09_, A.D. _2014_.

Certificate

№ CS-005

For 2 Shares

Issued to

▮▮▮▮▮▮▮▮

Dated 09.01.2014

№ Original Certificate
№ Original Shares
№ Shares Transferred

Received Certificate No. CS-005

For 2 Shares

This 1st day of September, 2014

▮▮▮▮▮▮▮▮

For Value Received, _____ hereby sell, assign and transfer unto
_____
_____ Shares represented by the within
~~Certificate, and do hereby irrevocably~~ constitute and appoint
_____ Attorney to transfer the said Shares on
~~the books of the within named~~ Corporation with full power of substitution in
the premises.
Dated _____
In presence of
_____   _____

Corporate Seal — RK Engineering Works

№ CS-004 Shares 2

RK ENGINEERING WORKS, INC.

This Certifies that ▇▇▇▇ is the registered holder of _2_ Shares of the Capital Stock transferable only on the books of the Corporation by the holder hereof in person or by Attorney upon surrender of this Certificate properly endorsed.

In Witness Whereof, the said Corporation has caused this Certificate to be signed by its duly authorized officers and its Corporate Seal is to be hereunto affixed this _01_ day of _09_, A.D. _2014_.

Certificate

No ___CS-004___

For ___2___ Shares

Issued to

[REDACTED]

Dated ___09.01.2014___

№. Original Certificate

№. Original Shares

№. Shares Transferred

Received Certificate No. ___CS-004___

For ___2___ Shares

This ___1st___ day of September, 2014

[REDACTED]

_____

For Value Received, _____ hereby sell, assign and transfer unto
_____
_____ Shares represented by the within
Certificate, and do hereby irrevocably constitute and appoint
_____ Attorney to transfer the said Shares on
the books of the within named Corporation with full power of substitution in
the premises.
Dated _____
In presence of

_____   _____

№ CS-003								Shares 2

RK ENGINEERING WORKS, INC.

This Certifies that ▮▮▮ *is the registered holder of* 2 *Shares of the Capital Stock, transferable only on the books of the Corporation by the holder hereof in person, or by Attorney upon surrender of this Certificate properly endorsed.*

In Witness Whereof, the said Corporation has caused this Certificate to be signed by its duly authorized officers and its Corporate Seal is to be hereunto affixed this 01 *day of* 09 *, A.D.* 2014 :

Certificate

№ CS-003

For 2 Shares

Issued to

▮▮▮▮▮▮▮▮▮▮

Dated 09.01.2014

7b. Original Certificate
7b. Original Shares
7b. Shares Transferred

Received Certificate No. CS-003

For 2 Shares

This 1st day of September, 2014

▮▮▮▮▮▮▮▮▮▮

For Value Received, _____ hereby sell, assign and transfer unto
_____
_____ Shares represented by the within Certificate, and do hereby irrevocably constitute and appoint _____ Attorney to transfer the said Shares on the books of the within named Corporation with full power of substitution in the premises.
Dated _____
In presence of
_____ _____

№ CS-002　　　　　　　　　　　　　　　　　　　　Shares　2

RK ENGINEERING WORKS, INC.

This Certifies that ▬▬▬ *is the registered holder of* 2 *Shares of the Capital Stock, transferable only on the books of the Corporation by the holder hereof in person or by Attorney upon surrender of this Certificate properly endorsed.*

In Witness Whereof, the said Corporation has caused this Certificate to be signed by its duly authorized officers and its Corporate Seal is to be hereunto affixed this 01 *day of* 09 *, A.D.* 2014 *.*

Certificate

№ CS-002

For 2 Shares

Issued to

▬▬▬▬▬

Dated 09 01, 2014

R. Original Certificate
Th. Original Shares
M. Shares Transferred

Received Certificate No. CS-002

For 2 Shares

This 1st day of September, 2014

▬▬▬▬▬

_____

For Value Received, _____ hereby sell, assign and transfer unto

_____

_____ Shares represented by the within Certificate, and do hereby irrevocably constitute and appoint _____ Attorney to transfer the said Shares on the books of the within named Corporation with full power of substitution in the premises.

Dated _____

In presence of

_____   _____

№ CS-001　　　　　　　　　　　　　　　　　　　　Shares 2

RK ENGINEERING WORKS, INC.

This Certifies that ▮ *is the registered holder of* 2 *Shares of the Capital Stock, transferable only on the books of the Corporation by the holder hereof in person or by Attorney upon surrender of this Certificate properly endorsed.*

In Witness Whereof, the said Corporation has caused this Certificate to be signed by its duly authorized officers and its Corporate Seal is to be hereunto affixed this 01 day of 09, A.D. 2014.

Certificate

№ CS-001

For 2 Shares

Issued to

▉▉▉▉▉▉

Dated 09.01.2014

₦. Original Certificate
₦. Original Shares
₦. Shares Transferred

Received Certificate №. CS-001

For 2 Shares

This 1st day of September, 2014

▉▉▉▉▉▉▉▉▉▉

For Value Received, _____ hereby sell, assign and transfer unto

_____

_____ Shares represented by the within Certificate, and do hereby irrevocably constitute and appoint
_____ Attorney to transfer the said Shares on the books of the within named Corporation with full power of substitution in the premises.

Dated _____

In presence of

_____ _____

[RK Engineering Works California C 3690907 Corporate Seal]

Source of Funds

Commonwealth Bank
Commonwealth Bank of Australia
ABN 48 123 123 124

24/05/2014

[REDACTED]

[REDACTED]

Your Variable Rate Personal Loan

Thank you for applying for a Variable Rate Personal Loan. Your application has been conditionally approved, subject to our normal verification checks. That means we need a little more information from you before we can finalise your application.

Here are the details of your loan:

[loan details box — illegible]

Your loan documents

We have enclosed important information about your loan, including your Contract Schedule and our Usual Terms and Conditions for Consumer Lending booklet (which as of 1 January 2011 includes the Credit Guide). Together, these two documents will make up your loan Offer if your loan goes ahead, so it's important for you to read them carefully.

In particular, make sure you read Part G of the Terms and Conditions, "Things You Should Know about Your Proposed Credit Contract". It's also important to keep copies of these documents and your Direct Debit Request Service Agreement for future reference.

For your convenience, your Contract Schedule, along with other important documents, are also available in NetBank for you to view and accept.

What do you need to do?

To finalise your application, please log on to NetBank and go to **My Applications** to complete the following:

- Proof of income. If your salary has been paid into a Commonwealth Bank account for three months or more, then that's all the proof you need. Otherwise, please upload your last two payslips (no more than 60 days old). If you do not have payslips or you receive other forms of income, check the enclosed Income Document Guide for more information about what you need to do.

- If you have an existing CBA account which you've held for more than 6 months, please upload your most recent statement for any accounts you hold with other financial institutions, including transaction/savings account, loans and credit cards.

- Otherwise, if you have no CBA accounts or have held your CBA account for less than 6 months, please upload your most recent three months statements for any accounts you hold with other financial institutions, including savings accounts, loans and credit card.

- View and accept your Contract Schedule. If you would like something changed, please contact us.

- Accept your Loan Account Authority form.

- Accept your Direct Debit Request form.

If you are not registered for NetBank, you can go to netbank.com.au to register. Alternatively, please sign and return the documents listed in the Document Checklist to any of our branches.

Please be sure to accept/provide us all of the documents we need within one month of the Disclosure Date set out in your Contract Schedule. Otherwise, this approval will expire and we will need to begin the process again.

What happens next?

By accepting/signing your Contract Schedule, you are making an offer to the Commonwealth Bank to enter into a loan contract.

We are not obliged to accept your offer or make the money available until we have received and checked your documents — so it's important to get them to us as soon as you can.

Once your application has been finalised, we'll be in touch to confirm the outcome.

We're here to help

If you have any questions or need more information, please log on to netbank.com.au/my applications or call 13 14 31 between 8am and 8pm, Sydney time 7 days a week.

Yours sincerely,

Brian Moseley
General Manager
Retail Customer Service

Signed for and on behalf of Commonwealth Bank of Australia by
BRIAN MOSELEY on the 24th day of May 2014

Your acceptance: When you sign or electronically accept this Schedule, you make an offer, as set out in the Schedule and the UTC, and acknowledge that any Security stated at Item K extends to cover your obligations under the Contract.

IMPORTANT

BEFORE YOU SIGN OR ACCEPT

- READ THE CONTRACT DOCUMENTS so that you know exactly what contract you are entering into and what you will have to do under the Contract.
- Unless your Loan is provided wholly or predominantly for investment (other than in residential property) or business purposes (or for both purposes), you should also read the information statement: THINGS YOU SHOULD KNOW ABOUT YOUR PROPOSED CREDIT CONTRACT.
- Fill in or cross out any blank spaces.
- Get a copy of the contract documents.
- Do not sign this contract document if there is anything you do not understand.

THINGS YOU MUST KNOW

- You can withdraw this offer at any time before the credit provider accepts it. When the credit provider does accept it, you will be bound by it. However, you may end the Contract before you obtain credit or a card or other means is used to obtain goods or services for which credit is to be provided under the Contract, by telling the Bank (the Bank is your credit provider) in writing, but you will still be liable for any fees or charges already incurred.
- You do not have to take out consumer credit insurance unless you want to. If the Contract or mortgage document says so, you must take out insurance over any mortgaged property.
- If you are taking out insurance, the Bank cannot insist on any particular insurance company.
- If this Contract document says so, the Bank can vary the annual percentage rate (the interest rate), the repayments and the fees and charges and can add new fees and charges without your consent.
- If the Contract says so, the Bank can charge a fee if you pay out your contract early.

Note: You do not have to physically sign this document, if we have provided it to you electronically and agreed you can accept it electronically, in the way we specify.

BANK USE ONLY	Application Number : 96102172001
Received by the Bank on the .... day of .... year	
Signature/s verified and confirmed by:	
Staff name	Staff number ....
Signature	Date ....

PAGE 99

Commonwealth Bank
Commonwealth Bank of Australia
ABN 48 123 123 124

International Money Transfer (Customer Copy)

Section 1 - IMT details

Lodging branch BSB	Lodging branch name	IMT reference number	Date
2223	PARRAMATTA	[redacted]	02-OCT-2014

Destination Country	USA	Foreign Currency Amount	USD	24,397.44
Dealer number		Exchange Rate		0.8384000
		AUD Amount		29,100.00
		Fee		30.00
		Total amount Paid		29,130.00

Section 2 - Sender details

Sender's full name & residential address: [redacted]

Sender's account number: [redacted]

CIF Number: [redacted]

Section 3 - Beneficiary details

Beneficiary's full name & residential address:
RK ENGINEERING WORKS
[redacted]

Description/purpose of payment: [redacted]

Beneficiary's bank name and address:
JPMORGAN CHASE BANK N A

NEW YORK NY
USA

Beneficiary's bank code: [redacted]

Beneficiary's account number / IBAN: [redacted]

Intermediary bank name and address:
NOT APPLICABLE

Intermediary bank code: [ ]

[Stamp: 02 OCT 2014 PARRAMATTA COMMONWEALTH BANK]

Section 4 - Terms and Conditions

The Sender (you) agrees:
1. We (the Bank) may use overseas banks to process this transaction.
2. Money sent overseas is usually available for payment to the beneficiary within two business days (Australian time) of our accepting your instructions.
3. We are not liable for:
   - any loss suffered as a result of us acting on these instructions in good faith except where our negligence causes the loss; or
   - any delays in payment to the beneficiary by overseas banks.
4. Overseas banks may charge processing fees which they may deduct from the payment. If an overseas bank separately charges us a processing fee you must reimburse us for that fee. We can give you an estimate of the fees but the actual amounts can vary and may be significant.
5. Overseas banks may convert the currency sent into other currencies. In some cases, they may first convert Australian dollars to an intermediate currency (such as U.S. dollars or Euros) prior to conversion to the desired ending currency. This could happen even where the desired ending currency is Australian dollars.
6. You must pay us our fees, and any costs we incur to make enquiries to overseas banks regarding payment as set out in our brochure Standard fees and Charges for International and Foreign Currency Services.
7. We may decline to process this transaction if we believe in good faith that processing the transaction may breach laws, e.g. relating to anti-money laundering.
8. We collect personal info to: identify you for the Anti-Money Laundering/CTF Act; share with third parties to complete transactions; or use it as per our Privacy Policy (which includes how to access, correct or provide feedback on your info).
9. If funds are to be returned, they will be done so at the prevailing daily rates on the day of return.
10. If any provision of this agreement is found to be illegal, void or unenforceable for unfairness or any other reason, the remaining provisions of this agreement will continue to apply to the extent possible as if the void or unenforceable provision never existed.

PAGE 100

Commonwealth Bank
Commonwealth Bank of Australia
ABN 48 123 123 124

International Money Transfer (Customer Copy)

Section 1 - IMT details

Lodging branch BSB	Lodging branch name	IMT reference number	Date
2223	PARRAMATTA	[redacted]	30-SEP-2014

Destination Country: USA
Dealer number:

Foreign Currency Amount	USD	18,372.20
Exchange Rate		0.8351000
AUD Amount		22,000.00
Fee		30.00
Total amount Paid		22,030.00

Section 2 - Sender details

Sender's full name & residential address: [redacted]
Sender's account number: [redacted]
CIF Number: [redacted]

Section 3 - Beneficiary details

Beneficiary's full name & residential address:
[redacted] WORKS
UNIT 3
LOS ANGELES CA 90034 USA

Description/purpose of payment:
ROUTING 322271627
SHARES INVESTING

Beneficiary's bank name and address:
JPMORGAN CHASE BANK N A
NEW YORK NY
USA

Beneficiary's bank code: [redacted]
Beneficiary's account number / IBAN: [redacted]

Intermediary bank name and address:
NOT APPLICABLE

Intermediary bank code:

Section 4 - Terms and Conditions

The Sender (you) agrees:
1. We (the Bank) may use overseas banks to process this transaction.
2. Money sent overseas is usually available for payment to the beneficiary within two business days (Australian time) of us accepting your instructions.
3. We are not liable for:
   - any loss suffered as a result of us acting on these instructions in good faith except where our negligence causes the loss; or
   - any delays in payment to the beneficiary by overseas banks.
4. Overseas banks may charge processing fees which they may deduct from the payment. If an overseas bank separately charges us a processing fee you must reimburse us for that fee. We can give you an estimate of the fees but the actual amounts can vary and may be significant.
5. Overseas banks may convert the currency sent into other currencies. In some cases, they may first convert Australian dollars to an intermediate currency (such as U.S. dollars or Euros) prior to conversion to the desired ending currency. This could happen even where the desired ending currency is Australian dollars.

6. You must pay us our fees, and any costs we incur to make enquiries to overseas banks regarding payment as set out in our brochure Standard fees and Charges for International and Foreign Currency Services.
7. We may decline to process this transaction if we believe in good faith that processing the transaction may breach laws, e.g. relating to anti-money laundering.
8. We collect personal info to: identify you for the Anti-Money Laundering/CTF Act; share with third parties to complete transactions; or use it as per our Privacy Policy (which includes how to access, correct or provide feedback on your info).
9. If funds are to be returned, they will be done so at the prevailing daily rates on the day of return.
10. If any provision of this agreement is found to be illegal, void or unenforceable for unfairness or any other reason, the remaining provisions of this agreement will continue to apply to the extent possible as if the void or unenforceable provision never existed.

Holding Escrow Instructions

Tower Escrow Inc.
3800 Wilshire Blvd., Suite 426
Los Angeles, CA 90010

Phone: (213) 386-6800
Fax: (213) 386-6801

Please find below Wiring Instructions for Escrow No. L-032867-KP

All funds wired should be directed to:

Bank	Uniti Bank
Address	3327 Wilshire Blvd., Suite A
City/State	Los Angeles, CA 90010
ABA	
Credit to	TOWER ESCROW INC.
Account No.	
Swift Code	
Reference	Katie Park, Escrow Officer Escrow No. L-032867-KP

If you have any questions regarding this matter, please do not hesitate to contact this office.

Please Note: Not all electronic funds transfers are the same.

An ACH transfer is not a bank wire transfer.

Tower Escrow Inc. cannot accept ACH (Automated Clearing House) transfers for escrow deposits and all such transfers will be rejected and returned. As a result, close of escrow will be delayed by ACH transfers. Only wire transfers (FedWire or CHIPS) from participating financial institutions will be honored.

Tower Escrow Inc.

Tower Escrow Inc.
3600 Wilshire Blvd., Suite 426
Los Angeles, CA 90010

Phone: (213) 368-6800
Fax: (213) 368-6801

TOWER ESCROW INC. IS LICENSED BY THE DEPARTMENT OF BUSINESS OVERSIGHT
OF THE STATE OF CALIFORNIA, LICENSE NUMBER 963-1916

HOLDING ESCROW INSTRUCTIONS

TO: Tower Escrow Inc.

Date: March 17, 2015
Escrow Officer: Katie Park
Escrow No.: L-032867-KP

▓▓▓▓▓▓ WORKS, INC. (hereinafter known as Party(ies), hereby agrees to provide this instruction for the escrow holder, Tower Escrow Inc., (hereinafter known as Escrow Holder).

HOLDING Consideration $23,000.00

INSTRUCTIONS TO ESCROW:

1. **PURPOSE OF ESCROW:** The party has opened this escrow, as part of an E-2 Business Visa application with United States Citizenship and Immigration Services (USCIS). The party shall deposit the sum of $23,000.00 into Tower Escrow Inc. upon signing herein and further provide written authorization of releasing funds from the funds deposited into escrow, along with an invoice indicating payee's information.

2. **ESCROW HOLDER'S DUTIES:** The party hereby agree and acknowledge that the escrow holder's only duty and performance in this escrow, shall be (a) to accept funds made by the party and (b) to release funds according to the Party's written instruction with invoice of payment. The Party is aware and fully acknowledge that all other procedures and/or documentation relating E-2 business visa application shall be handled by the Party and will not be a part of this escrow service. In the event that the escrow holder is requested to act or perform any other matters, than the escrow holder's duties as described in 2-(a) (b) hereinabove, the escrow holder has right to terminate this escrow unilaterally and return the Party's deposit funds, less escrow fees.

3. **ESCROW FEES:** The basic escrow fee shall be $500.00; provided that total disbursements are 10 (vendors) or less. If there are more than 10 disbursements, there will be additional fee of $35.00 for regular mailing or $50 for wiring, each disbursement. Any overnight mail or courier service fees, if needed or requested, shall be additionally charged.

4. **TERMINATION OF ESCROW:** The party, at any time, may terminate this escrow in writing. When written termination is given by the Party, the escrow holder shall terminate this escrow, without further cancellation instruction, and return the Party's deposit, less $350.00 cancellation fee, back to the Party.

5. **HOLD HARMLESS:** The Party hereby holds the escrow holder harmless and relieved of any liability and/or responsibility for complying with this instruction and the Party's written instruction within the escrow holder's duties as indicated herein.

The Party acknowledges that only applicable provisions from the following General Provisions, shall be applied toward this escrow.

ADDITIONAL ESCROW INSTRUCTIONS AND PROVISIONS

1. The parties to this escrow are made aware that Escrow Holder has no obligation to verify signatures of any of the parties involved.

2. You shall not be responsible for the following: (1) the sufficiency of correctness as to form, manner of execution or validity of any documents deposited in this escrow; (2) the identity, authority, or right of any person executing the same, either as to documents of record or those handled in this escrow; or (3) the failure of any party to comply with any of the provisions of any agreement, contract or other instrument filed or deposited in this escrow or referred to in those escrow instructions. Your duties shall limited to the safekeeping of money and documents received by you as Escrow Holder and for the disposition in compliance with the written instructions accepted by you in this escrow. You shall not be required to take any action regarding the collection, maturity, or apparent outlaw of any obligations deposited with you unless otherwise instruction in writing.

(CONTINUED)

Seller's Initials: _____/_____   Page 1 of 5

Date: March 17, 2015

3. Where the assignment of any insurance policy from Seller to Buyer is concerned, Seller guarantees to you any insurance policy handed you in this escrow is policy in force, the policy has not been hypothecated and that all necessary premiums have been paid. You are authorized to execute on behalf of the parties assignments of interest in any insurance policy (other than title insurance policies) called for in this escrow, you are authorized to transmit for assignment any insurance policy to the insurance agent requesting that the insurer consent to such assignment, to request that a loss payee clause or such other endorsements as may be required be issued and to forward such policy to the lenders and entitled parties. You shall not be responsible for verifying the acceptance of the request for assignment and policy of insurance by the insurance company. The parties mutually agree that you will make no attempt to verify the receipt of the request for assignment by the issuing insurance company. All parties are placed on notice that if the insurance company should fail to receive the assignment, the issuing company may deny coverage for any loss suffered by Buyer. IT IS THE OBLIGATION OF THE INSURED OR THE INSURED'S REPRESENTATIVE TO VERIFY THE ISSUING COMPANY'S ACCEPTANCE OF THE ASSIGNMENT OF THE POLICY.

4. You are not to be held responsible in any way whatsoever for any personal property tax which may be assessed against any former or present owner of the subject property described in these escrow instructions, nor for the corporation or license tax of any corporation as a former or present owner.

5. If it is necessary, proper or convenient for the consummation of this escrow, you are authorized to deposit or have deposited funds or documents, or both, handed you under these escrow instructions with any duly authorized sub-escrow agent, including, but not limited to, any bank, trust company, title insurance company, title company, savings and loan association, or licensed escrow agent, subject to your order at or before close of escrow in connection with closing this escrow. Any such deposit shall be deemed a deposit under the meaning of these escrow instructions.

6. The parties to this escrow have satisfied themselves outside of escrow that the transaction covered by this escrow is not in violation of the Subdivision Map Act or any law regulation land division, zoning ordinances or building restrictions which may affect the land or improvements that are the subject of this escrow. You, as escrow holder, are relieved of all responsibility and liability in connection with such laws, ordinances, restrictions or regulations and are not to be concerned with any of their enforcement.

7. If any form of Purchase Agreement of amendment or supplement (collectively "Purchase Agreement") is deposited in this escrow, it is understood that such document shall be effective only as between the parties signing the Purchase Agreement. You, as Escrow Holder, are not to be concerned with the terms of any Purchase Agreement and are relieved of all responsibility for the enforcement of its terms. Your only duty is to comply with the instructions set forth in the escrow instructions. You are not responsible for interpreting or acting on any provision of any Purchase Agreement on which these escrow instructions may be based and you shall not rely on any knowledge or understanding you may have of any such Purchase Agreement in ascertaining or performing your duties as Escrow Holder. In connection with any loan transaction, you are authorized to deliver a copy of any Purchase Agreement, supplement or amendment and a copy of all escrow instructions, supplements or amendments to the lender.

8. You shall make no physical inspection of the real property or personal property described in any instruments deposited in, or which is the subject of this escrow. You have made no representations or warranties concerning any such real property or personal property and are not to be concerned with nor liable for the condition of real property or personal property.

9. The parties authorize the recordation of any instrument delivered through this escrow if necessary or proper for the issuance of the required policy of title insurance or for the closing of this escrow. Funds, instructions or instruments received in this escrow may be delivered to, or deposited with any title insurance company or title company to comply with the terms and conditions of this escrow.

10. You are to use your usual document forms or the usual forms of any title insurance company or title company and in our instructions insert dates and terms on the instruments if incomplete when executed.

11. If the date by which Buyer's or Seller's performances are due shall be other than your regular business day, such performances shall be due on your next succeeding business day.

12. You shall conduct no lien or title search of personal property regarding the sale or transfer of any personal property through this escrow. Should the parties desire that you conduct a lien or title search of personal property, the parties requesting the same shall deliver separate and specific written escrow instructions to you along with an agreement to pay your additional escrow fees.

13. You shall not be responsible in any way whatsoever nor are you to be concerned with any question of usury in any loan or encumbrance, whether new or of record, which may arise during the processing of this escrow.

14. The parties agree to deliver to you all documents, instruments, escrow instructions and funds required to process and close this escrow in accordance with its terms.

15. You are instructed to provide title to the subject real property in the condition identified in the escrow instructions by the parties. You are not responsible for the contents or accuracy of any beneficiary demands and/or beneficiary statements delivered to you by the existing lien-holders. You are not required to submit any such beneficiary statements and/or demand to the parties for approval before the close of escrow unless expressly instructed to do so in writing. Should the parties desire to pre-approve any such beneficiary statement and/or demand, the parties requesting the same shall deliver separate and specific written escrow instructions to you.

16. You are not to be responsible in any way whatsoever nor to be concerned with the terms of any new loan or the

(CONTINUED)

Seller's Initials: _____/_____

Date: March 17, 2015   Escrow No.: L-032807-KP

content of any loan documents obtained by any party in connection with this escrow except to order such loan documents into the escrow file, transmit the loan documents to Buyer for execution and transmit the executed loan documents to lender. The parties understand and agree that you are not involved nor concerned with the approval and/or processing of any loan or the contents and effect of loan documents prepared by a lender.

17. "NO ACTION SHALL LIE AGAINST ESCROW HOLDER FOR ANY CLAIMS, LOSS, LIABILITY, OR ALLEGED CAUSE OF ACTION OF ANY KIND OR NATURE WHATSOEVER, HOWEVER CAUSED OR OCCURRED UNDER THIS ESCROW, OR IN CONNECTION WITH THE HANDLING OR PROCESSING OF THIS ESCROW, UNLESS BROUGHT WITHIN TWELVE (12) MONTHS AFTER THE CLOSE OF ESCROW, OR A CANCELLATION, OR A TERMINATION OF THIS ESCROW FOR ANY REASON WHATSOEVER."

18. The parties expressly indemnify and hold you harmless against third-party claims for any fees, costs or expenses where you have acted in good faith, with reasonable care and prudence and/or in compliance with these escrow instructions. You are not required to submit any such beneficiary statement and/or beneficiary demand to the parties for approval before the close of escrow unless expressly instructed to do so in writing. Should the party(ies) desire to pre-approve any such beneficiary statement and/or beneficiary demand, the party(ies) requesting the same shall deliver separate and specific written escrow instructions to you.

19. The Federal Tax Reform Act of 1986, as amended, and the California Revenue & Taxation Code, require certain transactions to be reported to the Internal Revenue Service and the California State Franchise Tax Board. In those transactions Seller will furnish a correct tax identification number to you so you can report this transaction as required by law. Seller understands that Seller may be subject to civil or criminal penalties for failure to do so.

20. The parties agree that you have the responsibilities of an Escrow Holder only and there are no other legal relationships established in the terms and conditions of the escrow instructions. In connection with this escrow: (1) You shall have no duty or responsibility of notifying any of the parties to this escrow of any sale, resale, loan, exchange or other transaction involving any of the subject real property or personal property; (2) You shall have no responsibility or duty to disclose any benefit, including, but not limited to financial gain, realized by any person, firm or corporation involving any of the subject real property or personal property; and (3) You shall have no responsibility or duty to disclose any profit realized by any person, firm or corporation including, but not limited to, any real estate broker, real estate sales agent and/or a party to any other escrow, in connection therewith, although such other transaction may be handled by you in this escrow or in another escrow transaction. If, however, you are instructed in writing by any party, Lender or other entitled person to disclose any sale, resale, loan, exchange or other transaction involving any of the subject real property or personal property or any profit realized by any person, firm or corporation to any party to this escrow, you shall do so without incurring any liability to any party. You shall not be liable for any of your acts or omissions done in good faith nor for any claims, demands, losses or damages made or suffered by any party to this escrow, excepting such as may arise through or be caused by your willful neglect or gross misconduct.

21. Buyer acknowledges that pursuant to the California Revenue & Taxation Code a Change of Ownership form is required by the county recorder to be completed and affixed to any documents submitted for recording which evidence a conveyance of title. The Change of Ownership form shall be furnished to Buyer by you for Buyer's completion and execution. Buyer is aware that if Buyer does not complete the form in full, sign and return it to you before closing, a penalty will be assessed by the county recorder. If the Change of Ownership form is not filed after the close of escrow within the time limits set forth by the county recorder, severe additional penalties will be assessed against the Buyer.

For information and assistance in completing the Change of Ownership form, Buyer may contact the County Recorder and Assessors offices in the county in which the subject property is located.

22. The parties shall cooperate with you in carrying out the escrow instructions they deposit with you and completing this escrow. The parties shall deposit into escrow, upon request, any additional funds, instruments, documents, instructions, authorizations, or other items that are necessary to enable you to comply with demands made on you by third parties, to secure policies of title insurance, or to otherwise carry out their instructions and close this escrow. If conflicting demands or notices are made or served upon you or any controversy arises between the parties or with any third person arising out of or relating to this escrow, you shall have the absolute right to withhold and stop all further proceedings in, and in performance of, this escrow until you receive written notification satisfactory to you of the settlement of the controversy by written agreement of the parties, or by the final order or judgment of a court of competent jurisdiction.

All of the parties to this escrow, jointly and severally, promise to pay promptly on demand, as well as to indemnify you and to hold you harmless from and against all administrative governmental investigations, audit and legal fees, litigation and interpleader costs, damages, judgments, attorneys' fees, arbitration costs and fees, expenses, obligations and liabilities of every kind (collectively "costs") which in good faith you may incur or suffer in connection with or arising out of this escrow, whether said costs arise during the performance of or subsequent to this escrow, directly or indirectly, and whether at trial, or on appeal, in administrative action, or in an arbitration. You are given a lien upon all the rights, titles and interests of the parties and all escrow papers and other property and monies deposited into this escrow to protect your rights and to indemnify and reimburse you. If the parties do not pay any fees, costs or expenses due you under the escrow instructions or do not pay for costs and attorneys' fees incurred in any litigation, administrative action and/or arbitration, on demand, they each agree to pay a reasonable fee for any attorney services which may be required to collect such fees or expenses, whether attorneys' fees are incurred before trial, at trial, on appeal or in arbitration.

23. ALL NOTICES, DEMANDS AND INSTRUCTIONS MUST BE IN WRITING. No notice, demand, instruction, amendment, supplement or modification of these escrow instructions shall be of any effect in this escrow until delivered in writing to you and mutually executed by all parties.

Any purported oral instruction, amendment, supplement, modification, notice
(CONTINUED)

Seller's Initials: _____/_____   Page 3 of 5

Date: March 17, 2015   Escrow No.: L-032887-KP

parties or either of them shall be ineffective and invalid. You are to be concerned only with the directives expressly set forth in the escrow instructions, supplements and amendments thereto, and are not to be concerned with nor liable for items designated as "memorandum items" in the escrow instructions. These escrow instructions may be executed in counterparts, each of which shall be deemed an original regardless of the date of its execution and delivery. All such counterparts together shall constitute the same document.

The parties acknowledge and understand that you, as Escrow Holder, are not authorized to practice the law nor do you give financial advice. The parties are advised to seek legal and financial counsel and advice concerning the effect of these escrow instructions. The parties acknowledge that no representations are made by you about the legal sufficiency, legal consequences, financial effects or tax consequences of the within escrow transaction.

24. Notwithstanding any other provisions in these escrow instructions and in addition to other fees and costs to which you may be entitled, the parties, jointly and severally, agree that if this escrow is not consummated within ninety (90) days of the date set for closing, you are instructed to, and without further instructions, withhold your escrow hold open fee of $50.00 per month from the funds on deposit with you regardless of who deposited such funds. The parties, jointly and severally, further agree that if you are, for any reason, required to hold funds after close of escrow, you are instructed to, and without further instructions, withhold an escrow fee of $50.00 per month from the funds on deposit with you regardless of who deposited such funds. The parties irrevocably instruct you to automatically cancel this file without further instructions when all funds on deposit have been disbursed.

25. Your Escrow Holder agency shall terminate six (6) months following the date last set for close of escrow and shall be subject to earlier termination by receipt by you of mutually executed cancellation instructions. If this escrow was not closed or cancelled within the described six (6) month period, you shall have no further obligations as Escrow Holder except to disburse funds and documents pursuant to written escrow instructions and to interplead or otherwise dispose of funds and documents in accordance with a validly issued and validly served order from a court of competent jurisdiction. If the conditions of this escrow have not been complied with at the expiration date in these escrow instructions, you are instructed to complete the conditions at the earliest possible date, unless Buyer or Seller have made written demand upon you for the return of the funds and/or instruments deposited by Buyer or Seller and/or for cancellation of this escrow.

Should demands be made upon you, you may withhold and stop all further proceedings in this escrow without liability for interest on funds held or for damages until mutual cancellation instructions signed by all parties shall have been deposited with you. The parties, jointly and severally, agree that if this escrow cancels or is otherwise terminated and not closed, the parties shall pay for any costs and expenses which you have incurred or have become obligated for under these escrow instructions, including, but not limited to, attorneys' fees, arbitration fees and costs and reasonable escrow fees for the services rendered by you, the parties agree that such costs and expenses shall be paid and deposited in escrow before any cancellation or other termination of this escrow is effective. The parties agree that said charges for expenses, costs and fees may be apportioned between Buyer and Seller in a manner which, in your sole discretion, you consider equitable, and that your decision will be binding and conclusive upon the parties. Upon receipt of mutual cancellation instructions or a final order or judgment of a court of competent jurisdiction with accompanying writs of execution, levies or garnishments, you are instructed to disburse the escrow funds and instruments in accordance with such cancellation instruction, order or judgment and accompanying writ and this escrow shall, without further notice be considered terminated and cancelled.

26. If any check submitted to you is dishonored upon presentment for payment, you are authorized to notify all parties to the within escrow, their respective real estate brokers and real estate agents and any other person or entity you deem in you sole discretion necessary to notify.

27. The parties agree to release you from any and all liability of any kind or nature and to indemnify you from any loss, damages, claims, judgments or costs of any kind or nature resulting from or related to the release or discharge of hazardous or toxic wastes on the subject property whether it occurred in the past or present or may occur in the future which release or discharge is in violation of law, in excess of any state and federal standards, permit requirements and/or disclosure requirements existing at this time or which may exist at a future time. The parties represent that they made their own assessment of the condition of the subject property and have not relied on any of your representations in making the assessment. The parties are advised to seek independent legal and technical environmental expert advice in assessing the risks associated with potential hazardous or toxic wastes.

28. In these escrow instructions, wherever the context so requires, the masculine gender includes the feminine and/or neuter and the singular number includes the plural.

29. You are authorized to destroy or otherwise dispose of any and all documents, papers, escrow instructions, correspondence and records or other material constituting or pertaining to this escrow at any time after five (5) years from the date of: (1) the close of escrow; (2) the date of cancellation; or (3) the date of the last activity without liability and without further notice to the parties.

(CONTINUED)

Seller's Initials: _____ / _____

Date: March 17, 2015   Escrow No.: L-032867-KP

WE, JOINTLY AND SEVERALLY, ACKNOWLEDGE RECEIPT OF A COMPLETE COPY OF THE WITHIN ESCROW INSTRUCTIONS AND BY OUR SIGNATURES SET FORTH BELOW, ACKNOWLEDGE THAT WE HAVE READ, UNDERSTAND AND AGREE TO BE BOUND BY WE TERMS AND CONDITIONS CONTAINED THEREIN, IN THEIR ENTIRETY.

The foregoing terms, provisions, conditions and instructions are hereby approved and accepted in their entirety and concurred with by me. I will hand you necessary documents called for on my part to cause title to be shown as set out herein, which you are authorized to deliver when you hold or have caused to be applied to funds set forth herein within the time as herein provided. You are authorized to pay on my behalf, my recording fees, charges for evidence of title as called for whether or not this escrow is consummated, except those the buyer agreed to pay. You are hereby authorized to pay bonds, assessments, taxes, and any liens of record, including prepayment penalties, if any, to show title as called for.

You are further instructed to pay documentary transfer tax on deed as required.

BUYERS:

RK ENGINEERING WORKS, INC., a California Corporation

#3, Los Angeles, CA 90034 (USA)
4/3 Elizabeth St, Artarmon, NSW 2064 Australia

Tower Escrow Inc
3600 Wilshire Blvd., Suite 426
Los Angeles, CA 90010
(213) 368-6800

03 - Uniti Bank

RECEIPT NO. 38746

ESCROW NO.

DATE 03/18/2015

Property: HOLDING ESCROW

RECEIVED OF ███████ WORKS

AMOUNT
$*****23,500.00

TWENTY-THREE THOUSAND FIVE HUNDRED AND 00/100 DOLLARS

	ABA Number	Check Number	Description
CASH			
CHECK			
CASHIER'S CHECK			
OTHER	WIRE		

Checking Account Number _____ Received on behalf of BUYER/BORROWER

BY DEBORAH WON

ORIGINAL

I HEREBY CERTIFY THAT THIS IS A TRUE AND EXACT COPY OF THE ORIGINAL

FedPayments Manager℠ – Funds

Delivered to FPM:	03/18/2015 14:54:27	Test/Prod:	Prod
IMAD:	20150318 B1QGC07C 005223 03181454		
OMAD:	20150318 QMGFNP72 001772 03181454		

BASIC INFORMATION
Sender ABA {3100}: 021000021 JPMORGAN CHASE
Receiver ABA {3400}: 122243415 UNITI BK BUSHA PK
Amount {2000}: 23,500.00
Type/Subtype Code (1510): 1000 - Transfer of Funds
Business Function {3600}: CTR - Customer Transfer
Sender Reference {3320}: 337250007788
Reference for Beneficiary (4320): BOH OF 15/03/18

ORIGINATOR INFORMATION
Originator (5000)
  ID Code: D - DDA Account Number
  Identifier: 629593653
  Name: RK ENGINEERING WORKS
  Address: 1000 MACDONALD AVE APT 120
    RICHMOND, CA 948013151

BENEFICIARY INFORMATION
Beneficiary (4200)
  ID Code: D - DDA Account Number
  Identifier: 002317220
  Name: TOWER ESCROW INC.
  Address: 3327 WILSHIRE BLVD SUITE A
    LOS ANGELES CA 90010 US

I HEREBY CERTIFY THAT THIS IS A TRUE AND EXACT COPY OF THE ORIGINAL

03/18/2015 14:56:54

032867-kp

Letter to Escrow Company

Ms Katie Park
Senior Escrow Officer
TOWER ESCROW INC.
3600 Wilshire Blvd., Suite 426
Los Angeles, CA 90010
Phone: (213)-368-6800
Fax: (213)368-6801
Re.: Establishment of Holding Escrow account for E-2 visa

March 9th, 2015

Dear Ms. Park,

It is with pleasure that ████████ Director and Principal Engineer – ██ ████████ Works, Inc., hereby inform you that our company have decided to engage Tower Escrow Inc. (i.e. your company) to provide escrow services required as part of an E-2 business visa application with United States Citizenship and Immigration Services (USCIS). This document has been prepared to discuss the scope of service, method of funds transfer, condition of funds holding, conditions for funds release and other issues.

Scope of Service
Tower Escrow is to open a holding escrow account to hold funds for transfer to vendors for computer software, hardware and furniture purchases that are to be made if the E-2 visa is approved by USCIS. The holding escrow account is to be opened for the following party (i.e. our company):

████████ Works, Inc.
████████ #3
Los Angeles, CA 90034
USA.
Phone: (562)508-4917

Pursuant to our earlier communication, Statement of Information for the Corporation filed with the California Secretary's office is included in Appendix A.

Funds Transfer Method
The funds to be held in the escrow account would be transferred from our company business account, which is with Chase Bank of California. We will make a wire transfer from our account to a nominated account of Tower Escrow Inc. We request that the following bank information is provided for this purpose:
- Bank routing number
- Account number

Instructions for Tower Escrow Inc.
Establishment of holding escrow

If above information is not available, please inform us of an alternate method of funds transfer (agreeable to both parties) and related information.

Conditions of Funds Holding

The fund in the holding escrow account is expected to be available in the holding escrow account until our company has been granted a decision by USCIS for the E-2 business visa application.

Conditions of Funds Release

As this is a holding escrow account, the funds are to be held in the account until we inform you (in writing) of one of the two outcomes, as stated below.

Outcome No. 1

Application for E-2 visa is approved by USCIS. Funds to be released by your company to the parties identified in Vendor Schedules included in Appendix B. The vendor schedules identify each item to be purchased and price information, as was obtained from the vendors (or their websites). Official price quotes from some of the vendors have been included in Appendix B. These quotes also indicate the acceptable methods of payment. If unsure, please discuss with me or directly contact the vendors for confirmation of funds release method. For the purchases to be made from IKEA (furniture) and Fry's Electronics (MISC. Software), we request that you provide me or a nominated representative of our company with two company checks or money orders payable to Fry's electronics and IKEA in the total amount shown in the vendor schedule.

Outcome No. 2

Application for E-2 visa is not approved by USCIS. The escrow account is to be dissolved and entire amount held in the escrow account is returned to our company account via a wire transfer. Our company bank account information will be forwarded to you at that time so that you are able to make the funds transfer promptly.

What we need from you

To start the escrow account establishment and funds transfer, we need the following information from your company:

1. Acceptable method of funds transfer from our company account to Tower Escrow.

2. Your company bank information so that a wire transfer from our company account can be made to your selected bank account.

3. Written confirmation that your company fees are to be $500.00 for the escrow services. Please also provide information regarding additional

Instructions for Tower Escrow Inc.
Establishment of holding escrow

fees if more than 10 vendor transfers are made. We do not, however, anticipate more than 10 vendor transfers at this point. Please provide confirmation of funds transfer and escrow account establishment documentation from your company which will be included in the visa application.

4. Acceptable methods of notification to your company from our company to convey the outcome of the E-2 visa application.
5. Time frame to return the funds from the escrow account to our business account in case E-2 visa is not approved.
6. Any other limitations that Tower Escrow may have.

We would like to thank you again for your assistance in this matter. Our Attorney, Law offices of Brian Lerner of Long Beach, California, is awaiting the escrow documentation. As such, we would request that you take action leading to the establishment of the escrow account as soon as possible.

Sincerely,

APPENDIX A

-Corporation Establishment Filing

14-071662

State of California
Secretary of State
Statement of Information
(Domestic Stock and Agricultural Cooperative Corporations)
FEES (Filing and Disclosure): $25.00.
If this is an amendment, see instructions.
IMPORTANT -- READ INSTRUCTIONS BEFORE COMPLETING THIS FORM

75 S

FILED
Secretary of State
State of California
SEP 0 9 2014

Ref $4 9/15/14
35/25/CC/4R

1. CORPORATE NAME: ███ Works

2. CALIFORNIA CORPORATE NUMBER: 3690837

No Change Statement. (Not applicable if agent address of record is a P.O. Box address. See instructions.)
- If there have been any changes to the information contained in the last Statement of Information filed with the California Secretary of State, or no statement of information has been previously filed, this form must be completed in its entirety.
- ☐ If there has been no change in any of the information contained in the last Statement of Information filed with the California Secretary of State, check the box and proceed to Item 17.

Complete Addresses for the Following (Do not abbreviate the name of the city. Items 4 and 5 cannot be P.O. Boxes.)

		CITY	STATE	ZIP CODE
4. STREET ADDRESS OF PRINCIPAL EXECUTIVE OFFICE ███ #3		Los Angeles	CA	90034
5. STREET ADDRESS OF PRINCIPAL BUSINESS OFFICE IN CALIFORNIA, IF ANY: As above		CITY	CA	ZIP CODE
6. MAILING ADDRESS OF CORPORATION, IF DIFFERENT THAN ITEM 4		CITY	STATE	ZIP CODE

Names and Complete Addresses of the Following Officers (The corporation must list these three officers. A comparable title for the specific officer may be added; however, the preprinted titles on this form must not be altered.)

	ADDRESS	CITY	STATE	ZIP CODE
7. CHIEF EXECUTIVE OFFICER/ ███				
8. SECRETARY ███	1000 Macdonald Avenue #120	Richmond	CA	94801
9. CHIEF FINANCIAL OFFICER/ ███				

Names and Complete Addresses of All Directors, Including Directors Who are Also Officers (The corporation must have at least one director. Attach additional pages, if necessary.)

	ADDRESS	CITY	STATE	ZIP CODE
10. NAME				
11. NAME				
12. NAME				

13. NUMBER OF VACANCIES ON THE BOARD OF DIRECTORS, IF ANY:

Agent for Service of Process If the agent is an individual, the agent must reside in California and Item 15 must be completed with a California street address, a P.O. Box address is not acceptable. If the agent is another corporation, the agent must have on file with the California Secretary of State a certificate pursuant to California Corporations Code section 1505 and Item 15 must be left blank.

14. NAME OF AGENT FOR SERVICE OF PROCESS: Faruk Sharif

15. STREET ADDRESS OF AGENT FOR SERVICE OF PROCESS IN CALIFORNIA, IF AN INDIVIDUAL CITY ███ STATE CA ZIP CODE 91324

Type of Business

16. DESCRIBE THE TYPE OF BUSINESS OF THE CORPORATION: Enginering Consultancy

17. BY SUBMITTING THIS STATEMENT OF INFORMATION TO THE CALIFORNIA SECRETARY OF STATE, THE ███ CONTAINED HEREIN, INCLUDING ANY ATTACHMENTS, IS TRUE AND CORRECT.

08/25/2014 — DATE
███ — Director — TITLE

SI-200 (REV 01/2013)

I hereby certify that the foregoing
transcript of _____/_____ page(s)
is a full, true and correct copy of the
original record in the custody of the
California Secretary of State's office.

SEP 18 2014

Date: _____

Debra Bowen
DEBRA BOWEN, Secretary of State

APPENDIX B

- Vendor Schedules
- Official Vendor Quotes

VENDOR SCHEDULE #1 (Engineering Software purchase)

Item No.	Software Name	Vendor Name/Address/Contact	Quote Ref. #	Price (US$)	Acceptable Payment Methods
1	AutoCAD for MAC 2015	MICRODESK 523 W 6th Street #516 Los Angeles, CA 90014 United States 1-800-336-3375 Eric Massey	OID: 1-RGV24	$3,825.49	Credit card
2	Slide	ROCSCIENCE #780-439 University Avenue, Toronto, Ontario M5G 1Y8 Canada Ph: (416)698-8217 Anthony Salvalaggio	Invoice # 9743	$2,570.00	Bank wire transfer Check Credit card
3	Plaxis	PLAXIS Plaxis Americas LLC 2500 Wilcrest Drive, Suite #300, Houston, TX 77042	Ref. #S04256314 Quote # 00001385	$10,350.00	Bank Wire Wells Fargo Bank
4	Gint	BENTLEY SYSTEMS, INCORPORATED 685 Stockton Drive, Exton, PA 19341 Ph: 1 800 513 5103 Email: bac@bentley.com Linda Gibb Bentley Account Manager (610) 458-5000	Quote #40603948	$927.00	Bank wire Check

VENDOR SCHEDULE #1 (Engineering Software purchase)

Item No.	Software Name	Vendor Name/Address/Contact	Quote Ref. #	Price (US$)	Acceptable Payment Methods
5	LiquefyPro	Civiltech Software 18707 SE Newport Way #406 Issaquah, WA 98027 Ph: 888-812-9525 Fax: 425-998-0145	Invoice #41117	$910.00	Check
6	Group	ENSOFT Inc. 3003 West Howard Lane Austin, TX 78728 Ph: (512)-244-6464 Fax: (512)-244-6067 sales@ensoftinc.com	Quote No. 7459	$1,800.00	Wire Transfer Credit Card Purchase Order
		Engineering Software purchase Total		$20,382.49	

Note: Vendor schedule #1 includes vendors that need to be paid individually. The payment methods are indicative only, and it is requested that Tower Escrow determine the most economical payment option from the vendor.

VENDOR SCHEDULE #2 (Misc. Software purchase from Fry's Electronics)

Item No.	Software Name	Vendor Name/Address/Contact	Quote Ref. #	Price (US$)	Acceptable Payment Methods
7A	Microsoft Office 2011 for MAC	Fry's Electronics	In-store purchase	$219	Check to Fry's electronics
7B	Esset Cyber Security (MAC)	Fry's Electronics	In-store purchase	$39.99	Check to Fry's electronics
7C	Quickbooks for MAC 2015	Fry's Electronics	In-store purchase	$299.95	Check to Fry's electronics
7D	Soda pdf Professional	Fry's Electronics	In-store purchase	$79.99	Check to Fry's electronics
			Misc. Software purchase Total	$638.93	

Note: It is expected that all items in schedule #2 can be purchased with one company check from Tower Escrow. The check can be provided to myself or a nominat528ed representative of ▓▓▓▓▓▓ Works, Inc.

VENDOR SCHEDULE #3 (Computer additional hardware purchase from Fry's Electronics)

Item No.	Hardware Type/Name	Vendor Name/Address/Contact	Quote Ref. #	Price (US$)	Acceptable Payment Methods
8A	Firewall VPN Firewall gateway VFG6005 Series Gigabit VPN ZYXEL Communications Inc Model VFG6005N	Fry's Electronics	In-store purchase	$114.99	Check to Fry's electronics
8B	Router D-Link DIR-810L Wireless-AC750 Dual Band Cloud Router Model DIR-810L	Fry's Electronics	In-store purchase	$69.99	Check to Fry's electronics
8C	Backup Storage Device HGST-Western Digital 4TB Thunderbolt Model #0G03050	Fry's Electronics	In-store purchase	$379.99	Check to Fry's electronics
8D	Printer/Copier/Scanner Samsung Multifunction Xpress C460FW Color Laser printer	Fry's Electronics	In-store purchase	$399.99	Check to Fry's electronics
		Computer additional hardware purchase Total		$964.96	

Note: It is expected that all items in schedule #3 can be made with a check made out to Fry's electronics.

VENDOR SCHEDULE #4 (office furniture purchase from IKEA)

Item No.	Furniture Type/Model	Vendor Name/Address/Contact	Quote Ref. #	Price (US$)	Acceptable Payment Methods
9A	Desk Ikea Desk with pull out Panel x2 units Malm 602.141.83	IKEA	In-store purchase	$298.00	Check to IKEA
9B	Swivel Chair Markus Swivel Chair x2 units 001.031.02	IKEA	In-store purchase	$398.00	Check to IKEA
9C	Bookcase-Storage Kalax Shelving unit with doors 990.171.86	IKEA	In-store purchase	$94.99	Check to IKEA
9D	File Cabinet Erik File cabinet x2 units	IKEA	In-store purchase	$198.00	Check to IKEA
		IKEA Office Furniture Purchase Total		$988.99	

Note: It is expected that all items in schedule #4 can be made with a check made out to IKEA.

Lease Agreements

Lease Agreement

1. Term.

A. Celia B. Lerner (Landlord) hereby leases the [REDACTED] Works, Inc. (Tenant), and Tenant hereby leases the same from Landlord, for an "Initial Term" beginning ~~September~~ OCTOBER 1, 2014 and (2K) ending month to month. If Tenant wants possession prior to the first of the month, then Tenant will pay the pro-rata portion for the remainder of the current month. Landlord shall use its best efforts to give Tenant possession as nearly as possible at the beginning of the Lease term. If Landlord is unable to timely provide the Leased Premises, rent shall abate for the period of delay. Tenant shall make no other claim against Landlord for any such delay.

B. Tenant may renew the Lease. The monthly rent for the leased premises shall be raised for inflation 5% per year. Whether Tenant renews the lease for a year, or goes month to month, there shall be a 5% increase in the rent on the annual expiration of the lease. The renewal term shall be at the rental set forth below and otherwise upon the same convenants, conditions and provisions as provided in this Lease.

2. Rental.

A. Tenant shall pay to Landlord during the Initial Term rental of $550 per month, payable by the 3rd of every month. If payment is not received by the third of every month, there will be a $25 late charge. Each payment shall be paid to Celia Lerner and placed in her mail bin on the first floor of the building at 3233 E. Broadway, Long Beach, California 90803. Tenant shall also pay to Landlord a "Security Deposit" in the amount of $275 along with the last months rent of the initial term in the amount of $550.00.

The initial payment shall consist of the first month, last month and security deposit.

3. Use

Notwithstanding the forgoing, Tenant shall not use the Leased Premises for the purposes of storing, manufacturing or selling any explosives, flammables or other inherently dangerous substance, chemical, thing or device.

4. Sublease and Assignment.

Tenant shall not have the right without Landlord's consent, to assign this Lease to a corporation with which Tenant may merge or consolidate, to any subsidiary of Tenant, to any corporation under common control with Tenant, or to a purchaser of substantially all of Tenant's assets. Except as set forth above,

Tenant shall not sublease all or any part of the Leased Premises, or assign this Lease in whole or in part without Landlord's consent, such consent not to be unreasonably withheld or delayed.

5. Copies and use of Copy Machine

Landlord has a high speed copier and scanner on the first floor of the building. Tenant will receive a code to use the copier. At the end of every month, Tenant will be billed 20 cents for every copy made during the month.

6. Alterations and Improvements.

Tenant shall have the right to place and install personal property, trade fixtures, equipment and other temporary installations in and upon the Leased Premises, and fasten the same to the premises. All personal property, equipment, machinery, trade fixtures and temporary installations, whether acquired by Tenant at the commencement of the Lease term or placed or installed on the Leased Premises by Tenant thereafter, shall remain Tenant's property free and clear of any claim by Landlord. Tenant shall have the right to remove the same at any time during the term of this Lease provided that all damage to the Leased Premises caused by such removal shall be repaired by Tenant at Tenant's expense.

7. Property Taxes.

Landlord shall pay, prior to delinquency, all general real estate taxes and installments of special assessments coming due during the Lease term on the Leased Premises, and all personal property taxes with respect to Landlord's personal property, if any, on the Leased Premises. Tenant shall be responsible for paying all personal property taxes with respect to Tenant's personal property at the Leased Premises.

8. Internet Usage.

The rental unit will have access to high speed wireless internet. If Tenant wants to have access to the internet, the cost will be $45.00 per month.

9. Utilities.

Tenant shall pay all charges for telephone, installation of the telephone, and other items specifically related to the use of the telephone used by Tenant on the Leased Premises during the term of this Lease unless otherwise expressly agreed in writing by Landlord.

10. Signs.

There is no specific signage for Tenant.

11. Entry.

Landlord shall have the right to enter upon the Leased Premises at reasonable hours to inspect the same, provided Landlord shall not thereby unreasonably interfere with Tenant's business on the Leased Premises.

12. Parking.

During the term of this Lease, Tenant shall have the non-exclusive use in common with Landlord, other tenants of the Building, their guests and invitees, of the non-reserved common automobile parking areas, driveways, and footways, subject to rules and regulations for the use thereof as prescribed from time to time by Landlord. Landlord reserves the right to designate parking areas within the Building or in reasonable proximity thereto, for Tenant and Tenant's agents and employees. Tenant shall provide Landlord with a list of all license numbers for the cars owned by Tenant, its agents and employees.

13. Building Rules.

Tenant will comply with the rules of the Building adopted and altered by Landlord from time to time and will cause all of its agents, employees, invitees and visitors to do so; all changes to such rules will be sent by Landlord to Tenant in writing. The initial rules for the Building are attached hereto as Exhibit "A" and incorporated herein for all purposes.

14. Damage and Destruction.

Subject to Section 8 A. above, if the Leased Premises or any part thereof or any appurtenance thereto is so damaged by fire, casualty or structural defects that the same cannot be used for Tenant's purposes, then Tenant shall have the right within ninety (90) days following damage to elect by notice to Landlord to terminate this Lease as of the date of such damage. In the event of minor damage to any part of the Leased Premises, and if such damage does not render the Leased Premises unusable for Tenant's purposes, Landlord shall promptly repair such damage at the cost of the Landlord. In making the repairs called for in this paragraph, Landlord shall not be liable for any delays resulting from strikes, governmental restrictions, inability to obtain necessary materials or labor or other matters which are beyond the reasonable control of Landlord. Tenant shall be relieved from paying rent and other charges during any portion of the Lease term that the Leased Premises are inoperable or unfit for occupancy, or use, in whole or in part, for Tenant's purposes. Rentals and other charges paid in advance for any such periods shall be credited on the next ensuing payments, if any, but if no further payments are to be made, any such advance payments shall be refunded to Tenant. The provisions of this paragraph extend not only to the matters aforesaid, but also to any occurrence which is beyond Tenant's reasonable control and which renders the Leased Premises, or any appurtenance thereto, inoperable or unfit for occupancy or use, in whole or in part, for Tenant's purposes.

15. Default.

If default shall at any time be made by Tenant in the payment of rent when due to Landlord as herein provided, and if said default shall continue for fifteen (15) days after written notice thereof shall have been given to Tenant by Landlord, or if default shall be made in any of the other covenants or conditions to be kept, observed and performed by Tenant, and such default shall continue for thirty (30) days after notice thereof in writing to Tenant by Landlord without correction thereof then having been commenced and thereafter diligently prosecuted, Landlord may declare the term of this Lease ended and terminated by giving Tenant written notice of such intention, and if possession of the Leased Premises is not surrendered, Landlord may reenter said premises. Landlord shall have, in addition to the remedy above provided, any other right or remedy available to Landlord on account of any Tenant default, either in law or equity. Landlord shall use reasonable efforts to mitigate its damages.

16. Quiet Possession.

Landlord covenants and warrants that upon performance by Tenant of its obligations hereunder, Landlord will keep and maintain Tenant in exclusive, quiet, peaceable and undisturbed and uninterrupted possession of the Leased Premises during the term of this Lease.

17. Condemnation.

If any legally, constituted authority condemns the Building or such part thereof which shall make the Leased Premises unsuitable for leasing, this Lease shall cease when the public authority takes possession, and Landlord and Tenant shall account for rental as of that date. Such termination shall be without prejudice to the rights of either party to recover compensation from the condemning authority for any loss or damage caused by the condemnation. Neither party shall have any rights in or to any award made to the other by the condemning authority.

18. Subordination.

Tenant accepts this Lease subject and subordinate to any mortgage, deed of trust or other lien presently existing or hereafter arising upon the Leased Premises, or upon the Building and to any renewals, refinancing and extensions thereof, but Tenant agrees that any such mortgagee shall have the right at any time to subordinate such mortgage, deed of trust or other lien to this Lease on such terms and subject to such conditions as such mortgagee may deem appropriate in its discretion. Landlord is hereby irrevocably vested with full power and authority to subordinate this Lease to any mortgage, deed of trust or other lien now existing or hereafter placed upon the Leased Premises of the Building, and Tenant agrees upon demand to execute such further instruments subordinating this Lease or attorning to the holder of any such liens as Landlord may request. In the event that Tenant should fail to execute any instrument of subordination herein required to be executed by Tenant promptly as requested, Tenant hereby irrevocably constitutes Landlord as its attorney-in-fact to execute such instrument in Tenant's name, place and stead, it being agreed that such power is one coupled with an interest. Tenant agrees that it will from time to time upon request by Landlord execute and deliver to such persons as Landlord shall request a statement in recordable form certifying that this Lease is unmodified and in full force and effect (or if there have been modifications, that the same is in full force and effect as so modified), stating the dates to which rent and other charges payable under this Lease have been paid, stating that Landlord is not in default hereunder (or if Tenant alleges a default stating the nature of such alleged default) and further stating such other matters as Landlord shall reasonably require.

19. Security Deposit.

The Security Deposit shall be held by Landlord without liability for interest and as security for the performance by Tenant of Tenant's covenants and obligations under this Lease, it being expressly understood that the Security Deposit shall not be considered an advance payment of rental or a measure of Landlord's damages in case of default by Tenant. Unless otherwise provided by mandatory non-waivable law or regulation, Landlord may commingle the Security Deposit with Landlord's other funds. Landlord may, from time to time, without prejudice to any other remedy, use the Security Deposit to the extent necessary to make good any arrearages of rent or to satisfy any other covenant or obligation of Tenant hereunder. Following any such application of the Security Deposit, Tenant shall pay to Landlord on demand the amount so applied in order to restore the Security Deposit to its original amount. If Tenant is not in default at the termination of this Lease, the balance of the Security Deposit remaining after any such application shall be returned by Landlord to Tenant. If Landlord transfers its interest in the Premises during the term of this Lease, Landlord may assign the Security Deposit to the transferee and thereafter shall have no further liability for the return of such Security Deposit.

20. Notice.

Any notice required or permitted under this Lease shall be deemed sufficiently given or served if sent by United States certified mail, return receipt requested, addressed as follows:

If to Landlord to:

Celia B. Lerner
3233 E. Broadway
Long Beach, CA 90803

If to Tenant to:

Landlord and Tenant shall each have the right from time to time to change the place notice is to be given under this paragraph by written notice thereof to the other party.

21. Brokers.

Tenant represents that Tenant was not shown the Premises by any real estate broker or agent and that Tenant has not otherwise engaged in, any activity which could form the basis for a claim for real estate commission, brokerage fee, finder's fee or other similar charge, in connection with this Lease.

22. Waiver.

No waiver of any default of Landlord or Tenant hereunder shall be implied from any omission to take any action on account of such default if such default persists or is repeated, and no express waiver shall affect any default other than the default specified in the express waiver and that only for the time and to the extent therein stated. One or more waivers by Landlord or Tenant shall not be construed as a waiver of a subsequent breach of the same covenant, term or condition.

23. Memorandum of Lease.

The parties hereto contemplate that this Lease should not and shall not be filed for record, but in lieu thereof, at the request of either party, Landlord and Tenant shall execute a Memorandum of Lease to be recorded for the purpose of giving record notice of the appropriate provisions of this Lease.

24. Headings.

The headings used in this Lease are for convenience of the parties only and shall not be considered in interpreting the meaning of any provision of this Lease.

25. Successors.

The provisions of this Lease shall extend to and be binding upon Landlord and Tenant and their respective legal representatives, successors and assigns.

26. Consent.

Landlord shall not unreasonably withhold or delay its consent with respect to any matter for which Landlord's consent is required or desirable under this Lease.

27. Performance.

If there is a default with respect to any of Landlord's covenants, warranties or representations under this Lease, and if the default continues more than fifteen (15) days after notice in writing from Tenant to

Landlord specifying the default, Tenant may, at its option and without affecting any other remedy hereunder, cure such default and deduct the cost thereof from the next accruing installment or installments of rent payable hereunder until Tenant shall have been fully reimbursed for such expenditures, together with interest thereon at a rate equal to the lesser of twelve percent (12%) per annum or the then highest lawful rate. If this Lease terminates prior to Tenant's receiving full reimbursement, Landlord shall pay the unreimbursed balance plus accrued interest to Tenant on demand.

28. Compliance with Law.

Tenant shall comply with all laws, orders, ordinances and other public requirements now or hereafter pertaining to Tenant's use of the Leased Premises. Landlord shall comply with all laws, orders, ordinances and other public requirements now or hereafter affecting the Leased Premises.

29. Final Agreement.

This Agreement terminates and supersedes all prior understandings or agreements on the subject matter hereof. This Agreement may be modified only by a further writing that is duly executed by both parties. IN WITNESS WHEREOF, the parties have executed this Lease as of the day and year first above written.

Landlord

By: Celia B. Lerner

Date: August 19, 2014

Date: ~~August 19, 2014~~
Sept 24, 2014

Lease Agreement

1. Term.

A. Celia B. Lerner (Landlord) hereby leases the RK Engineering Works, Inc. (Tenant), and Tenant hereby leases the same from Landlord, for an "Initial Term" beginning April 1, 2015 and ending month to month. If Tenant wants possession prior to the first of the month, then Tenant will pay the pro-rata portion for the remainder of the current month. Landlord shall use its best efforts to give Tenant possession as nearly as possible at the beginning of the Lease term. If Landlord is unable to timely provide the Leased Premises, rent shall abate for the period of delay. Tenant shall make no other claim against Landlord for any such delay.

B. Tenant may renew the Lease. The monthly rent for the leased premises shall be raised for inflation 5% per year. Whether Tenant renews the lease for a year, or goes month to month, there shall be a 5% increase in the rent on the annual expiration of the lease. The renewal term shall be at the rental set forth below and otherwise upon the same convenants, conditions and provisions as provided in this Lease.

2. Rental.

A. Tenant shall pay to Landlord during the Initial Term rental of $850 per month, payable by the 3rd of every month. If payment is not received by the third of every month, there will be a $25 late charge. Each payment shall be paid to Celia Lerner and placed in her mail bin on the first floor of the building at 3233 E. Broadway, Long Beach, California 90803. Tenant shall also pay to Landlord a "Security Deposit" in the amount of $275 along with the last months rent of the initial term in the amount of $850.00.

The initial payment shall consist of the first month, last month and security deposit.

3. Use

Notwithstanding the forgoing, Tenant shall not use the Leased Premises for the purposes of storing, manufacturing or selling any explosives, flammables or other inherently dangerous substance, chemical, thing or device.

4. Sublease and Assignment.

Tenant shall not have the right without Landlord's consent, to assign this Lease to a corporation with which Tenant may merge or consolidate, to any subsidiary of Tenant, to any corporation under common control with Tenant, or to a purchaser of substantially all of Tenant's assets. Except as set forth above,

Tenant shall not sublease all or any part of the Leased Premises, or assign this Lease in whole or in part without Landlord's consent, such consent not to be unreasonably withheld or delayed.

5. Copies and use of Copy Machine

Landlord has a high speed copier and scanner on the first floor of the building. Tenant will receive a code to use the copier. At the end of every month, Tenant will be billed 20 cents for every copy made during the month.

6. Alterations and Improvements.

Tenant shall have the right to place and install personal property, trade fixtures, equipment and other temporary installations in and upon the Leased Premises, and fasten the same to the premises. All personal property, equipment, machinery, trade fixtures and temporary installations, whether acquired by Tenant at the commencement of the Lease term or placed or installed on the Leased Premises by Tenant thereafter, shall remain Tenant's property free and clear of any claim by Landlord. Tenant shall have the right to remove the same at any time during the term of this Lease provided that all damage to the Leased Premises caused by such removal shall be repaired by Tenant at Tenant's expense.

7. Property Taxes.

Landlord shall pay, prior to delinquency, all general real estate taxes and installments of special assessments coming due during the Lease term on the Leased Premises, and all personal property taxes with respect to Landlord's personal property, if any, on the Leased Premises. Tenant shall be responsible for paying all personal property taxes with respect to Tenant's personal property at the Leased Premises.

8. Internet Usage.

The rental unit will have access to high speed wireless internet. If Tenant wants to have access to the internet, the cost will be $45.00 per month.

9. Utilities.

Tenant shall pay all charges for telephone, installation of the telephone, and other items specifically related to the use of the telephone used by Tenant on the Leased Premises during the term of this Lease unless otherwise expressly agreed in writing by Landlord.

10. Signs.

There is no specific signage for Tenant.

11. Entry.

Landlord shall have the right to enter upon the Leased Premises at reasonable hours to inspect the same, provided Landlord shall not thereby unreasonably interfere with Tenant's business on the Leased Premises.

12. Parking.

During the term of this Lease, Tenant shall have the non-exclusive use in common with Landlord, other tenants of the Building, their guests and invitees, of the non-reserved common automobile parking areas, driveways, and footways, subject to rules and regulations for the use thereof as prescribed from time to time by Landlord. Landlord reserves the right to designate parking areas within the Building or in reasonable proximity thereto, for Tenant and Tenant's agents and employees. Tenant shall provide Landlord with a list of all license numbers for the cars owned by Tenant, its agents and employees.

13. Building Rules.

Tenant will comply with the rules of the Building adopted and altered by Landlord from time to time and will cause all of its agents, employees, invitees and visitors to do so; all changes to such rules will be sent by Landlord to Tenant in writing. The initial rules for the Building are attached hereto as Exhibit "A" and incorporated herein for all purposes.

14. Damage and Destruction.

Subject to Section 8 A. above, if the Leased Premises or any part thereof or any appurtenance thereto is so damaged by fire, casualty or structural defects that the same cannot be used for Tenant's purposes, then Tenant shall have the right within ninety (90) days following damage to elect by notice to Landlord to terminate this Lease as of the date of such damage. In the event of minor damage to any part of the Leased Premises, and if such damage does not render the Leased Premises unusable for Tenant's purposes, Landlord shall promptly repair such damage at the cost of the Landlord. In making the repairs called for in this paragraph, Landlord shall not be liable for any delays resulting from strikes, governmental restrictions, inability to obtain necessary materials or labor or other matters which are beyond the reasonable control of Landlord. Tenant shall be relieved from paying rent and other charges during any portion of the Lease term that the Leased Premises are inoperable or unfit for occupancy, or use, in whole or in part, for Tenant's purposes. Rentals and other charges paid in advance for any such periods shall be credited on the next ensuing payments, if any, but if no further payments are to be made, any such advance payments shall be refunded to Tenant. The provisions of this paragraph extend not only to the matters aforesaid, but also to any occurrence which is beyond Tenant's reasonable control and which renders the Leased Premises, or any appurtenance thereto, inoperable or unfit for occupancy or use, in whole or in part, for Tenant's purposes.

15. Default.

If default shall at any time be made by Tenant in the payment of rent when due to Landlord as herein provided, and if said default shall continue for fifteen (15) days after written notice thereof shall have been given to Tenant by Landlord, or if default shall be made in any of the other covenants or conditions to be kept, observed and performed by Tenant, and such default shall continue for thirty (30) days after notice thereof in writing to Tenant by Landlord without correction thereof then having been commenced and thereafter diligently prosecuted, Landlord may declare the term of this Lease ended and terminated by giving Tenant written notice of such intention, and if possession of the Leased Premises is not surrendered, Landlord may reenter said premises. Landlord shall have, in addition to the remedy above provided, any other right or remedy available to Landlord on account of any Tenant default, either in law or equity. Landlord shall use reasonable efforts to mitigate its damages.

16. Quiet Possession.

Landlord covenants and warrants that upon performance by Tenant of its obligations hereunder, Landlord will keep and maintain Tenant in exclusive, quiet, peaceable and undisturbed and uninterrupted possession of the Leased Premises during the term of this Lease.

17. Condemnation.

If any legally, constituted authority condemns the Building or such part thereof which shall make the Leased Premises unsuitable for leasing, this Lease shall cease when the public authority takes possession, and Landlord and Tenant shall account for rental as of that date. Such termination shall be without prejudice to the rights of either party to recover compensation from the condemning authority for any loss or damage caused by the condemnation. Neither party shall have any rights in or to any award made to the other by the condemning authority.

18. Subordination.

Tenant accepts this Lease subject and subordinate to any mortgage, deed of trust or other lien presently existing or hereafter arising upon the Leased Premises, or upon the Building and to any renewals, refinancing and extensions thereof, but Tenant agrees that any such mortgagee shall have the right at any time to subordinate such mortgage, deed of trust or other lien to this Lease on such terms and subject to such conditions as such mortgagee may deem appropriate in its discretion. Landlord is hereby irrevocably vested with full power and authority to subordinate this Lease to any mortgage, deed of trust or other lien now existing or hereafter placed upon the Leased Premises of the Building, and Tenant agrees upon demand to execute such further instruments subordinating this Lease or attorning to the holder of any such liens as Landlord may request. In the event that Tenant should fail to execute any instrument of subordination herein required to be executed by Tenant promptly as requested, Tenant hereby irrevocably constitutes Landlord as its attorney-in-fact to execute such instrument in Tenant's name, place and stead, it being agreed that such power is one coupled with an interest. Tenant agrees that it will from time to time upon request by Landlord execute and deliver to such persons as Landlord shall request a statement in recordable form certifying that this Lease is unmodified and in full force and effect (or if there have been modifications, that the same is in full force and effect as so modified), stating the dates to which rent and other charges payable under this Lease have been paid, stating that Landlord is not in default hereunder (or if Tenant alleges a default stating the nature of such alleged default) and further stating such other matters as Landlord shall reasonably require.

19. Security Deposit.

The Security Deposit shall be held by Landlord without liability for interest and as security for the performance by Tenant of Tenant's covenants and obligations under this Lease, it being expressly understood that the Security Deposit shall not be considered an advance payment of rental or a measure of Landlord's damages in case of default by Tenant. Unless otherwise provided by mandatory non-waivable law or regulation, Landlord may commingle the Security Deposit with Landlord's other funds. Landlord may, from time to time, without prejudice to any other remedy, use the Security Deposit to the extent necessary to make good any arrearages of rent or to satisfy any other covenant or obligation of Tenant hereunder. Following any such application of the Security Deposit, Tenant shall pay to Landlord on demand the amount so applied in order to restore the Security Deposit to its original amount. If Tenant is not in default at the termination of this Lease, the balance of the Security Deposit remaining after any such application shall be returned by Landlord to Tenant. If Landlord transfers its interest in the Premises during the term of this Lease, Landlord may assign the Security Deposit to the transferee and thereafter shall have no further liability for the return of such Security Deposit.

20. Notice.

Any notice required or permitted under this Lease shall be deemed sufficiently given or served if sent by United States certified mail, return receipt requested, addressed as follows:

If to Landlord to:

Celia B. Lerner
3233 E. Broadway
Long Beach, CA 90803

If to Tenant to:

███████ Works, Inc.
c/o ███ Khan
3233 E. Broadway
Long Beach, CA 90803

Landlord and Tenant shall each have the right from time to time to change the place notice is to be given under this paragraph by written notice thereof to the other party.

21. Brokers.

Tenant represents that Tenant was not shown the Premises by any real estate broker or agent and that Tenant has not otherwise engaged in, any activity which could form the basis for a claim for real estate commission, brokerage fee, finder's fee or other similar charge, in connection with this Lease.

22. Waiver.

No waiver of any default of Landlord or Tenant hereunder shall be implied from any omission to take any action on account of such default if such default persists or is repeated, and no express waiver shall affect any default other than the default specified in the express waiver and that only for the time and to the extent therein stated. One or more waivers by Landlord or Tenant shall not be construed as a waiver of a subsequent breach of the same covenant, term or condition.

23. Memorandum of Lease.

The parties hereto contemplate that this Lease should not and shall not be filed for record, but in lieu thereof, at the request of either party, Landlord and Tenant shall execute a Memorandum of Lease to be recorded for the purpose of giving record notice of the appropriate provisions of this Lease.

24. Headings.

The headings used in this Lease are for convenience of the parties only and shall not be considered in interpreting the meaning of any provision of this Lease.

25. Successors.

The provisions of this Lease shall extend to and be binding upon Landlord and Tenant and their respective legal representatives, successors and assigns.

26. Consent.

Landlord shall not unreasonably withhold or delay its consent with respect to any matter for which Landlord's consent is required or desirable under this Lease.

27. Performance.

If there is a default with respect to any of Landlord's covenants, warranties or representations under this Lease, and if the default continues more than fifteen (15) days after notice in writing from Tenant to

Landlord specifying the default, Tenant may, at its option and without affecting any other remedy hereunder, cure such default and deduct the cost thereof from the next accruing installment or installments of rent payable hereunder until Tenant shall have been fully reimbursed for such expenditures, together with interest thereon at a rate equal to the lessor of twelve percent (12%) per annum or the then highest lawful rate. If this Lease terminates prior to Tenant's receiving full reimbursement, Landlord shall pay the unreimbursed balance plus accrued interest to Tenant on demand.

28. Compliance with Law.

Tenant shall comply with all laws, orders, ordinances and other public requirements now or hereafter pertaining to Tenant's use of the Leased Premises. Landlord shall comply with all laws, orders, ordinances and other public requirements now or hereafter affecting the Leased Premises.

29. Final Agreement.

This Agreement terminates and supersedes all prior understandings or agreements on the subject matter hereof. This Agreement may be modified only by a further writing that is duly executed by both parties. IN WITNESS WHEREOF, the parties have executed this Lease as of the day and year first above written.

Landlord

By: Celia B. Lerner

Date: March 23, 2015

Date: March 23, 2015

Other Investments

Commonwealth Bank
Commonwealth Bank of Australia
ABN 48 123 123 124

International Money Transfer (Customer Copy)

Section 1 - IMT details

Lodging branch BSB	2223
Lodging branch name	PARRAMATTA
IMT reference number	M10IMT8024260-01
Date	08-JUL-2014
Destination Country	USA
Foreign Currency Amount	USD 6,000.00
Exchange Rate	0.8975000
AUD Amount	6,685.24
Fee	30.00
Total amount Paid	6,715.24

Section 2 - Sender details

Sender's full name & residential address: [redacted]
Sender's account number: [redacted]
CIF Number: [redacted]

Section 3 - Beneficiary details

Beneficiary's full name & residential address:
LAW OFFICE OF BRIAN D LERNER
LONG BEACH
CALIFORNIA USA

Description/purpose of payment: LEGAL SERVICES

Beneficiary's bank name and address:
WELLS FARGO BANK N A
SAN FRANCISCO PCS
SAN FRANCISCO CA
USA

Beneficiary's bank code: [redacted]
Beneficiary's account number / IBAN: [redacted]

Intermediary bank name and address: NOT APPLICABLE
Intermediary bank code:

Section 4 - Terms and Conditions

The Sender (you) agrees:

1. We (the Bank) may use overseas banks to process this transaction.
2. Money sent overseas is usually available for payment to the beneficiary within two business days (Australian time) of our accepting your instructions.
3. We are not liable for:
   - any loss suffered as a result of us acting on these instructions in good faith except where our negligence causes the loss; or
   - any delays in payment to the beneficiary by overseas banks.
4. Overseas banks may impose fees for processing payment to the beneficiary. Normally, these fees will be deducted by those banks from the payment. If however, the overseas banks charge us instead, you must reimburse us for such fees. You can ask us for the amount of these fees in advance. However the amount of these fees is not always known and may be significant.
5. Overseas banks may convert the currency sent into other currencies. In some cases, they may first convert Australian dollars to an intermediate currency (such as U.S. dollars or Euros) prior to conversion to the desired ending currency. This could happen even when
6. You must pay us our fees, and any costs we incur to make enquiries to overseas banks regarding payment as set out in our brochure Standard fees and Charges for International and Foreign Currency Services.
7. We may decline to process this transaction if we believe in good faith that processing the transaction may breach laws, e.g. relating to anti-money laundering.
8. You consent to the disclosure of the information in this Application to others (including overseas) as necessary to complete the transfer.
9. If funds are to be returned, they will be done so at the prevailing daily rates on the day of return.
10. If any provision of this agreement is found to be illegal, void or unenforceable for unfairness or any other reason (for example, if a court or other tribunal or authority declares it so), the remaining provisions of this agreement will continue to apply to the extent possible as if the void or unenforceable provision never existed.

Customer's signature: _____   Date: _____

DEALERSHIP GROUP

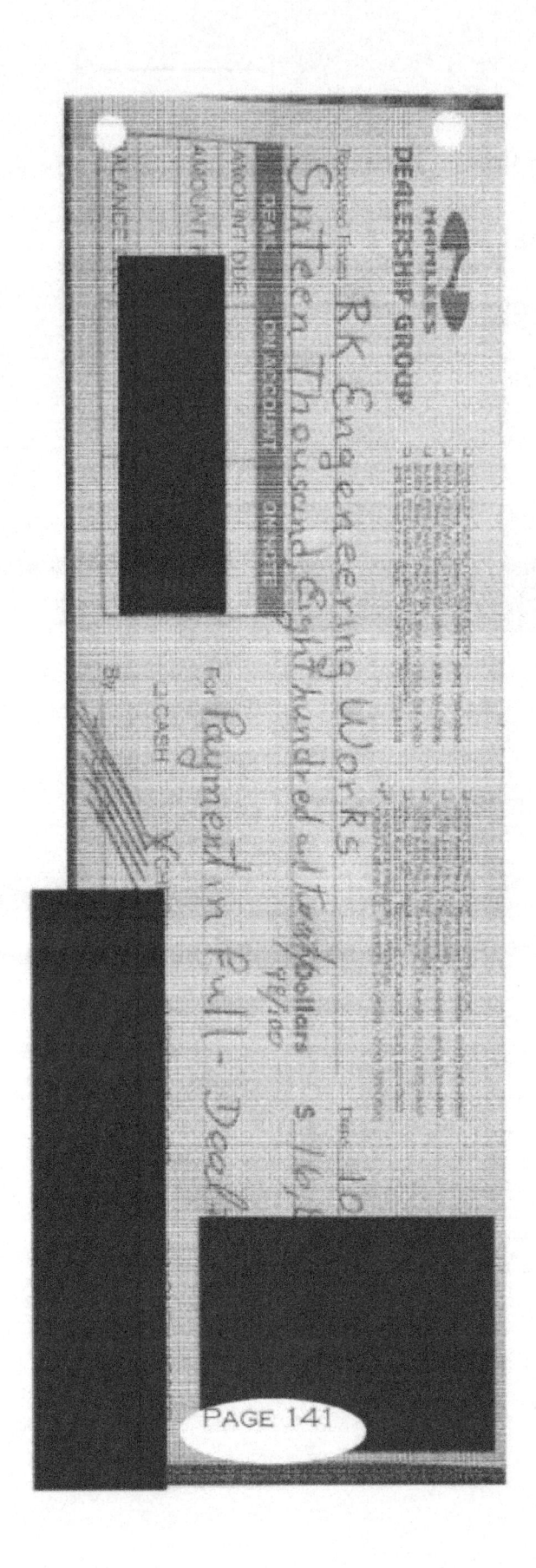

Received from RK Engineering Works

Sixteen Thousand Eight hundred and Twenty Dollars 98/100

$ 16,1...

For Payment in full - Deal...

☐ CASH

PAGE 141

RETAIL INSTALLMENT SALE CONTRACT – SIMPLE FINANCE CHARGE
(WITH ARBITRATION PROVISION)

Dealer Number: 4882 Contract Number: _____ R.O.S. Number: _____ Stock Number: G40B67

Buyer Name and Address (Including County and Zip Code)	Co-Buyer Name and Address (Including County and Zip Code)	Seller-Creditor (Name and Address)
RK ENGINEERING WORKS 1000 MACDONALD AVE APPT # 130 RICHMOND, CA 94801 CONTRA COSTA COUNTY		HILLTOP VOLKSWAGEN 3255 AUTO PLAZA RICHMOND, CA 94806

You, the Buyer (and Co-Buyer, if any), may buy the vehicle below for cash or on credit. By signing this contract, you choose to buy the vehicle on credit under the agreements on the front and back of this contract. You agree to pay the Seller - Creditor (sometimes "we" or "us" in this contract) the Amount Financed and Finance Charge in U.S. funds according to the payment schedule below. We will figure your finance charge on a daily basis. The Truth-In-Lending Disclosures below are part of this contract.

New/Used	Year	Make and Model	Odometer	Vehicle Identification Number	Primary Use For Which Purchased
NEW	2014	VOLKSWAGEN JETTA	11	3VW2K7AJ7EM445033	Personal, family or household unless otherwise indicated below. ☒ business or commercial

FEDERAL TRUTH-IN-LENDING DISCLOSURES

ANNUAL PERCENTAGE RATE The cost of your credit as a yearly rate.	FINANCE CHARGE The dollar amount the credit will cost you.	Amount Financed The amount of credit provided to you or on your behalf.	Total of Payments The amount you will have paid after you have made all payments as scheduled.	Total Sale Price The total cost of your purchase on credit, including your down payment of $ 0.00
0.00 %	$ 0.00 (e)	$ 16820.98	$ 16820.98 (e)	$ 16820.98 (e)

(e) means an estimate

STATEMENT OF INSURANCE
NOTICE. No person is required as a condition of financing the purchase of a motor vehicle to purchase or negotiate any insurance through a particular insurance company, agent or broker. You are not required to buy any other insurance to obtain credit. Your decision to buy or not buy other insurance will not be a factor in the credit approval process.

Vehicle Insurance
Term Premium
$ N/A Ded. Comp, Fire & Theft N/A Mos $ N/A
$ N/A Ded. Collision N/A Mos $ N/A
Bodily Injury $ N/A Limit N/A Mos $ N/A
Property Damage $ N/A Limit N/A Mos $ N/A
Medical N/A N/A Mos $ N/A
N/A N/A Mos $ N/A
Total Vehicle Insurance Premiums $ N/A

UNLESS A CHARGE IS INCLUDED IN THIS AGREEMENT FOR PUBLIC LIABILITY OR PROPERTY DAMAGE INSURANCE, PAYMENT FOR SUCH COVERAGE IS NOT PROVIDED BY THIS AGREEMENT.

You may buy the physical damage insurance this contract requires (see back) from anyone you choose who is acceptable to us. You are not required to buy any other insurance to obtain credit.

Buyer X RK ENGINEERING WORKS BY:
Co-Buyer X N/A
Seller X

If any insurance is checked below, policies or certificates from the named insurance companies will describe the terms and conditions.

YOUR PAYMENT SCHEDULE WILL BE:

Number of Payments:	Amount of Payments:	When Payments Are Due:
One Payment of	N/A	N/A
One Payment of	N/A	N/A
One Payment of	N/A	N/A
1	16820.98	Monthly beginning 10/13/2014
N/A	N/A	N/A
One final payment		N/A

Late Charge. If payment is not received in full within 10 days after it is due, you will pay a late charge of 5% of the part of the payment that is late.

		N/A	N/A
1		16820.98	Monthly beginning 10/13/2014
N/A	N/A	N/A	N/A
One final payment			

Late Charge. If payment is not received in full within 10 days after its due, you will pay a late charge of 5% of the part of the payment that is late.
Prepayment. If you pay off all your debt early, you may be charged a minimum finance charge.
Security Interest. You are giving a security interest in the vehicle being purchased.
Additional Information: See this contract for more information including information about nonpayment, default, any required repayment in full before the scheduled date, minimum finance charges, and security interest.

ITEMIZATION OF THE AMOUNT FINANCED (Seller may keep part of the amounts paid to others.)

1. **Total Cash Price**
   - A. Cash Price of Motor Vehicle and Accessories .... $ 15134.89 (A)
     1. Cash Price Vehicle .... $ 15134.89
     2. Cash Price Accessories .... $ N/A
     3. Other (Nontaxable)
        - Describe N/A .... $ N/A
        - Describe N/A .... $ N/A
   - B. Document Processing Charge (not a governmental fee) .. $ 80.00 (B)
   - C. Emissions Testing Charge (not a governmental fee) .... $ N/A (C)
   - D. (Optional) Theft Deterrent Device (to whom paid) N/A . $ N/A (D)
   - E. (Optional) Theft Deterrent Device (to whom paid) N/A . $ N/A (E)
   - F. (Optional) Theft Deterrent Device (to whom paid) N/A . $ N/A (F)
   - G. (Optional) Surface Protection Product (to whom paid) N/A .. $ N/A (G)
   - H. (Optional) Surface Protection Product (to whom paid) N/A .. $ N/A (H)
   - I. EV Charging Station (to whom paid) N/A .... $ N/A (I)
   - J. Sales Tax (on taxable items in A through I) .... $ 1369.34 (J)
   - K. Electronic Vehicle Registration or Transfer Charge
     (not a governmental fee) (to whom paid) GVR .... $ 29.00 (K)
   - L. (Optional) Service Contract (to whom paid) N/A ...... $ N/A (L)
   - M. (Optional) Service Contract (to whom paid) N/A ...... $ N/A (M)
   - N. (Optional) Service Contract (to whom paid) N/A ...... $ N/A (N)
   - O. (Optional) Service Contract (to whom paid) N/A ...... $ N/A (O)
   - P. (Optional) Service Contract (to whom paid) N/A ...... $ N/A (P)
   - Q. Prior Credit or Lease Balance paid by Seller to
     N/A .... (a) $ N/A (Q)
     (see downpayment and trade-in calculation)
   - R. (Optional) Gap Contract (to whom paid) N/A .... $ N/A (R)
   - S. (Optional) Used Vehicle Contract Cancellation Option Agreement $ N/A (S)
   - T. Other (to whom paid) N/A
     For N/A .... $ N/A (T)
   - Total Cash Price (A through T) .... $ 16613.23 (1)

2. **Amounts Paid to Public Officials**
   - ESTIMATE .... $ 99.00 (A)

You may buy the physical damage insurance this contract requires (see back) from anyone you choose who is acceptable to us. You are not required to buy any other insurance to obtain credit.

Buyer X RV ENGINEERING WORKS BY-
Co-Buyer X   N/A
Seller X

If any insurance is checked below, policies or certificates from the named insurance companies will describe the terms and conditions.

Application for Optional Credit Insurance
☐ Credit Life: ☐ Buyer ☐ Co-Buyer ☐ Both
☐ Credit Disability (Buyer Only)

	Term	Exp.	Premium
Credit Life	N/A	Mo N/A	$ N/A
Credit Disability	N/A	Mo N/A	$ N/A
Total Credit Insurance Premiums		$ N/A (B)

Insurance Company Name N/A
N/A
Home Office Address N/A
N/A

Credit life insurance and credit disability insurance are not required to obtain credit. Your decision to buy or not buy credit life and credit disability insurance will not be a factor in the credit approval process. They will not be provided unless you sign and agree to pay the extra cost. Credit life insurance is based on your original payment schedule. This insurance may not pay all you owe on this contract if you make late payments. Credit disability insurance does not cover any increase in your payment or in the number of payments. Coverage for credit life insurance and credit disability insurance ends on the original due date for the last payment unless a different term for the insurance is shown above.

You are applying for the credit insurance marked above. Your signature below means that you agree that: (1) You are not eligible for insurance if you have reached your 65th birthday. (2) You are eligible for disability insurance only if you are working for wages or profit 30 hours a week or more on the Effective Date. (3) Only the Primary Buyer is eligible for disability insurance. DISABILITY INSURANCE MAY NOT COVER CONDITIONS FOR WHICH YOU HAVE SEEN A DOCTOR OR CHIROPRACTOR IN THE LAST 6 MONTHS. (Refer to "Total Disabilities Not Covered" in your policy for details).
You want to buy the credit insurance.

Date	X N/A Buyer Signature	Age
Date	X N/A Co-Buyer Signature	Age

OPTIONAL GAP CONTRACT A gap contract (debt cancellation contract) is not required to obtain credit and will not be provided unless you sign below and agree to pay the extra charge. If you choose to buy a gap contract, the charge is shown in item 1R of the Itemization of Amount Financed. See your gap

Total Cash Price (A through T)	$ 16613.23	(1)
2. Amounts Paid to Public Officials		
A. Vehicle License Fees ESTIMATE	$ 98.00	(A)
B. Registration/Transfer/Titling Fees	$ 21.00	(B)
C. California Tire Fees	$ 8.75	(C)
D. Other SMOG ABATEMENT	$ 20.00	(D)
Total Official Fees (A through D)	$ 207.75	(2)
3. Amount Paid to Insurance Companies		
(Total premiums from Statement of Insurance column a + b)	$ N/A	(3)
4. ☐ State Emissions Certification Fee or ☐ State Emissions Exemption Fee	$ N/A	(4)
5. Subtotal (1 through 4)	$ 16820.98	(5)
6. Total Downpayment		
A. Agreed Trade-In Value Yr N/A Make N/A Model N/A Odom N/A VIN N/A	$ N/A	(A)
B. Less Prior Credit or Lease Balance (e)	$ N/A	(B)
C. Net Trade-In (A less B) (indicate if a negative number)	$ N/A	(C)
D. Deferred Downpayment	$ N/A	(D)
E. Manufacturer's Rebate	$ N/A	(E)
F. Other N/A	$ N/A	(F)
G. Cash	$ N/A	(G)
Total Downpayment (C through G)	$ 0.00	
(If negative, enter zero on line 6 and enter the amount less than zero as a positive number on line 1Q above)	Ø	
7. Amount Financed (5 less 6)	$	(7)

SELLER ASSISTED LOAN
BUYER MAY BE REQUIRED TO PLEDGE SECURITY FOR THE LOAN, AND WILL BE OBLIGATED FOR THE INSTALLMENT PAYMENTS ON BOTH THIS RETAIL INSTALLMENT SALE CONTRACT AND THE LOAN.

Proceeds of Loan From: _____ N/A _____
Amount $ _____ N/A _____ Finance Charge $ _____ N/A _____
Total $ _____ N/A _____ Payable in _____ N/A _____
Installments of $ _____ N/A _____ $ _____ N/A _____
from this Loan is shown in Item 6D.

AUTO BROKER FEE DISCLOSURE
If this contract reflects the retail sale of a new motor vehicle, the sale is not subject to a fee received by an autobroker from us unless the following box is checked:

☐ Name of autobroker receiving fee, if applicable:

OPTIONAL GAP CONTRACT A gap contract (debt cancellation contract) is not required to obtain credit and will not be provided unless you sign below and agree to pay the extra charge. If you choose to buy a gap contract, the charge is shown in Item 1R of the Itemization of Amount Financed. See your gap contract for details on the terms and conditions it provides. It is a part of this contract.
Term N/A Mos. N/A Name of Gap Contract
I want to buy a gap contract.
Buyer Signs X N/A

OPTIONAL SERVICE CONTRACT(S) You want to purchase the service contract(s) written with the following company(ies) for the term(s) shown below for the charge(s) shown in Items 1L, 1M, 1N, 1O, and/or 1P.
1L Company N/A
Term N/A Mos. or N/A Miles
1M Company N/A
Term N/A Mos. or N/A Miles
1N Company N/A
Term N/A Mos. or N/A Miles
1O Company N/A
Term N/A Mos. or N/A Miles
1P Company N/A
Term N/A Mos. or N/A Miles
Buyer X N/A

HOW THIS CONTRACT CAN BE CHANGED. This contract contains the entire agreement between you and us relating to this contract. Any change to the contract must be in writing and both you and we must sign it. No oral changes are binding.
Buyer Signs
Co-Buyer S

SELLER'S RIGHT TO CANCEL If Buyer and Co-Buyer sign here, the provisions of the Seller's Right to Cancel section on the back giving the Seller the right to cancel if Seller is unable to assign this contract to a financial institution will apply.

X _____ Buyer   X N/A Co-Buyer

Agreement to Arbitrate: By signing below, you agree that, pursuant to the Arbitration Provision on the reverse side of this contract, you or we may elect to resolve any dispute by neutral, binding arbitration and not by a court action. See the Arbitration Provision for additional information concerning the agreement to arbitrate.
Buyer Signs X _____   Buyer Signs X _____

OPTION: ☐ You pay no finance charge if the Amount Financed, Item 7, is paid in full on or before _____, Year _____ SELLER'S INITIALS _____

THE MINIMUM PUBLIC LIABILITY INSURANCE LIMITS PROVIDED IN LAW MUST BE MET BY EVERY PERSON WHO PURCHASES A VEHICLE. IF YOU ARE UNSURE WHETHER OR NOT YOUR CURRENT INSURANCE POLICY WILL COVER YOUR NEWLY ACQUIRED VEHICLE IN THE EVENT OF AN ACCIDENT, YOU SHOULD CONTACT YOUR INSURANCE AGENT.
WARNING:
YOUR PRESENT POLICY MAY NOT COVER COLLISION DAMAGE OR MAY NOT PROVIDE FOR FULL REPLACEMENT COSTS FOR THE VEHICLE BEING PURCHASED. IF YOU DO NOT HAVE FULL COVERAGE, SUPPLEMENTAL COVERAGE FOR COLLISION DAMAGE MAY BE AVAILABLE TO YOU THROUGH YOUR INSURANCE AGENT OR THROUGH THE SELLING DEALER. HOWEVER, UNLESS OTHERWISE SPECIFIED, THE COVERAGE YOU OBTAIN THROUGH THE DEALER PROTECTS ONLY THE DEALER, USUALLY UP TO THE AMOUNT OF THE UNPAID BALANCE REMAINING AFTER THE VEHICLE HAS BEEN REPOSSESSED AND SOLD.
FOR ADVICE ON FULL COVERAGE THAT WILL PROTECT YOU IN THE EVENT OF LOSS OR DAMAGE TO YOUR VEHICLE, YOU SHOULD CONTACT YOUR INSURANCE AGENT.
THE BUYER SHALL SIGN TO ACKNOWLEDGE THAT HE/SHE UNDERSTANDS THESE PUBLIC LIABILITY TERMS AND CONDITIONS.

WARNING

THE MINIMUM PUBLIC LIABILITY INSURANCE LIMITS PROVIDED IN LAW MUST BE MET BY EVERY PERSON WHO PURCHASES A VEHICLE. IF YOU ARE UNSURE WHETHER OR NOT YOUR CURRENT INSURANCE POLICY WILL COVER YOUR NEWLY ACQUIRED VEHICLE IN THE EVENT OF AN ACCIDENT, YOU SHOULD CONTACT YOUR INSURANCE AGENT.

YOUR PRESENT POLICY MAY NOT COVER COLLISION DAMAGE OR MAY NOT PROVIDE FOR FULL REPLACEMENT COSTS FOR THE VEHICLE BEING PURCHASED. IF YOU DO NOT HAVE FULL COVERAGE, SUPPLEMENTAL COVERAGE FOR COLLISION DAMAGE MAY BE AVAILABLE TO YOU THROUGH YOUR INSURANCE AGENT OR THROUGH THE SELLING DEALER. HOWEVER, UNLESS OTHERWISE SPECIFIED, THE COVERAGE YOU OBTAIN THROUGH THE DEALER PROTECTS ONLY THE DEALER, USUALLY UP TO THE AMOUNT OF THE UNPAID BALANCE REMAINING AFTER THE VEHICLE HAS BEEN REPOSSESSED AND SOLD.

FOR ADVICE ON FULL COVERAGE THAT WILL PROTECT YOU IN THE EVENT OF LOSS OR DAMAGE TO YOUR VEHICLE, YOU SHOULD CONTACT YOUR INSURANCE AGENT.

Buyer Signature X _____ Co-Buyer Signature X _____

Notice to buyer: (1) Do not sign this agreement before you read it or if it contains any blank spaces to be filled in. (2) You are entitled to a completely filled in copy of this agreement. (3) You can prepay the full amount due under this agreement at any time. (4) If you default in the performance of your obligations under this agreement, the vehicle may be repossessed and you may be subject to suit and liability for the unpaid indebtedness evidenced by this agreement.

If you have a complaint concerning this sale, you should try to resolve it with the seller.
Complaints concerning unfair or deceptive practices or methods by the seller may be referred to the city attorney, the district attorney, or an investigator for the Department of Motor Vehicles, or any combination thereof.
After this contract is signed, the seller may not change the financing or payment terms unless you agree in writing to the change. You do not have to agree to any change, and it is an unfair or deceptive practice...

Buyer Signature X _____ Co-Buyer Signature X _____

The Annual Percentage Rate may be negotiable with the Seller. The Seller may assign this contract and retain its right to receive a part of the Finance Charge.

THERE IS NO COOLING-OFF PERIOD UNLESS YOU OBTAIN A CONTRACT CANCELLATION OPTION	YOU AGREE TO THE TERMS OF THIS CONTRACT. YOU
California law does not provide for a "cooling-off" or other cancellation period for vehicle sales. Therefore, you cannot later cancel this contract simply because you change your mind, decide the vehicle costs too much, or wish you had acquired a different vehicle. After you sign below, you may only cancel this contract with the agreement of the seller or for legal cause, such as fraud. However, California law does require a seller to offer a two-day contract cancellation option on used vehicles with a purchase price of less than forty thousand dollars ($40,000), subject to certain statutory conditions. This contract cancellation option requirement does not apply to the sale of a recreational vehicle, a motorcycle, or an off-highway motor vehicle subject to identification under California law. See the vehicle contract cancellation option agreement for details.	CONFIRM THAT BEFORE YOU SIGNED THIS CONTRACT, WE GAVE IT TO YOU, AND YOU WERE FREE TO TAKE IT AND REVIEW IT. YOU ACKNOWLEDGE THAT YOU HAVE READ BOTH SIDES OF THIS CONTRACT, INCLUDING THE ARBITRATION PROVISION ON THE REVERSE SIDE, BEFORE SIGNING BELOW. YOU CONFIRM THAT YOU RECEIVED A COMPLETELY FILLED-IN COPY WHEN YOU SIGNED IT.

Buyer Signature X _____ Date _____ Co-Buyer Signature X _____ Date _____

Co-Buyers and Other Owners — A co-buyer is a person who is responsible for paying the entire debt. An other owner is a person whose name is on the title to the vehicle but does not have to pay the debt. The other owner agrees to the security interest in the vehicle given to us in this contract.

Other Owner Signature X _____ Address _____

GUARANTY: To induce us to sell the vehicle to Buyer, each person who signs as a Guarantor individually guarantees the payment of this contract. If Buyer fails to pay any money owing on this contract, each Guarantor must pay it when asked. Each Guarantor will be liable for the total amount owing even if other persons also sign as Guarantor, and even if Buyer has a complete defense to Guarantor's demand for reimbursement. Each Guarantor agrees to be liable even if we do one or more of the following: (1) give the Buyer more time to pay one or more payments; (2) give a full or partial release to any other Guarantor; (3) release any security; (4) accept less from the Buyer than the total amount owing; or (5) otherwise reach a settlement relating to this contract or extend the contract. Each Guarantor acknowledges receipt of a completed copy of this contract and guaranty at the time of signing.

Guarantor waives notice of acceptance of this Guaranty, notice of the Buyer's nonpayment, non-performance, and default, and notices of the amount owing at any time, and of any demands upon the Buyer.

Guarantor X _____ Date 10/15/14 Guarantor X _____ Date _____
Address _____ Address _____

Seller Signs _____ Date _____ By X _____ Title _____

CUSTOMER/TRUTH IN LENDING COPY

CHASE

Terms and Conditions (Remitter and Payee):

* Please keep this copy for your record of the transaction
* The laws of a specific state will consider these funds to be "abandoned" if the Cashier's Check is not cashed by a certain time
  - Please cash/deposit this Cashier's Check as soon as possible to prevent this from occurring
  - In most cases, the funds will be considered "abandoned" before the "Void After" Date
* Placing a Stop Payment on a Cashier's Check
  - Stop Payment can only be placed if the Cashier's Check is lost, stolen, or destroyed
  - We may not re-issue or refund the funds after the stop payment has been placed until 90 days after the original check was issued
* Please visit a Chase branch to report a lost, stolen, or destroyed Cashier's Check or for any other information about this item

FOR YOUR PROTECTION SAVE THIS COPY Customer Copy
CASHIER'S CHECK

10/11/2014
Void after 7 years

Remitter: RAFEL ZAFAR

Pay To The Order Of: HANLEES VW

Drawer: JPMORGAN CHASE BANK, N.A.
NON NEGOTIABLE

Memo:
Note: For information only. Comment has no effect on bank's payment.

MICRODESK

800-336-3375
team@microdesk.com
www.microdesk.com

March 3, 2015

OID: 1-RGV24

Dear ▮

I am pleased to present pricing for your review and consideration as follows:

Quantity	Product	Unit Price	Unit Total
1	AutoCAD for Mac 2015 New SLM ELD	$3,825.49	$3,825.49
1	AutoCAD for Mac 2015 Overview	0.00	0.00
	Total:		$3,825.49

Sales Tax and Shipping Additional
Pricing Valid Through <03/31/2015>

Training Services
Microdesk provides a variety of professionally-led training options including Autodesk Authorized Classroom Training (click here for the schedule of classes), Custom classroom, on-site and web based training. Please let me know if I can assist you in developing a training curriculum that meets your needs.

Technical Support
60 days of unlimited technical phone support is included with your purchase. Support hours are from 8am to 8pm EST Monday through Friday. Subscription customers receive unlimited technical phone support for the length of the contract.

Subscription - Budgeting for the Future
Subscription is an easy way to keep your design tools up to date, entitling you to automatically receive all updates and/or upgrades released for your software during your contract period. Please let me know if I can provide more information on Subscription or the valuable Subscription Center and e-learning tools included with it.

Business Process and Technology Consulting
With a team of more than 40 AECO professionals and software developers, our professional services group provides consulting to streamline operations, implement and standardize the use of technology, integrate applications and build solutions from the ground up. Please let me know how we can engage our professional services group to assist you and your firm.

Sincerely,

Eric Massey

PROPOSAL ACCEPTANCE:

To accept this proposal, please sign below and email to sgavini@microdesk.com at Microdesk, Inc. Receipt of this signed proposal indicates acceptance of the terms and conditions stated within and any additional terms or conditions submitted with this signed proposal do not apply.

*Sales Tax and shipping are additional – refer to invoice for total charges

Submitted and Accepted By:

_____   _____
Authorized Client Signature   Date

_____   _____
Print Name   P.O. # or Ref # (Please remit
                                                   copy with signed proposal)

Tax Exempt: ___Yes ___No (If yes please provide copy of exemption certificate)

Payment Method:

    ___ Credit Card (Please provide card info below)

    ___ 3rd Party Financing

    ___ Net 30 Terms (Prior credit approval required)

Credit Card Payment:

_____ _____ _____ _____
Card Number   Verification Code Exp Date   Card Type (Visa, Amx, etc.)

_____
Name on Card

_____
Billing Address for Name on Card

_____
City, State, Zip Code

Accounts Payable Contact (required):

_____
Name

_____
Email Address

_____
Telephone

GENERAL TERMS AND CONDITIONS

Pricing
Prices are subject to change without notice.

Payment Terms
Credit Card – All major cards accepted (Recommended Payment Option)
Financing (3rd Party Vendor with Prior Credit Approval)
Net 30 Terms (Prior Credit Approval Required)

Purchase Order Requirements
Terms must reflect **Net 30 days**, remittance should read:

Microdesk, Inc.
10 Tara Boulevard, Suite 420
Nashua, NH 03062

Refunds - 30 Day Return Policy on all Product and Subscription/Maintenance Orders except for Oracle Products and Oracle Subscriptions/Maintenance. Oracle Products and Oracle Subscription/Maintenance Orders are considered a final sale and nonrefundable.

Sales Tax
Applicable Sales Tax will be added to all orders.

> **Illinois, Maine, Massachusetts, New York, Pennsylvania, Rhode Island, Vermont and District of Columbia:**
> Microdesk will charge applicable sales tax for all product and subscription orders.
>
> **California, Maryland, New Jersey and Virginia:**
> Microdesk will _not_ charge sales tax for all electronically delivered product and subscription orders.
>
> If a media kit (physical media) is ordered via Microdesk, Microdesk is responsible for collecting sales tax for _all_ related media and subscription orders.
>
> If the end user requests physical media via Autodesk Subscription Center the end user is responsible for all applicable sales tax.
>
> **Connecticut:**
> Microdesk will charge full sales tax for all physically delivered product and new subscription orders.
>
> Microdesk will charge 1% sales tax for all electronically delivered orders and professional service orders.
>
> **Massachusetts:**
> Microdesk will charge full sales tax for all new product orders. Subscription and subscription renewals are 50% taxable.

Sales Tax Indemnification
Customers in California, Maryland, New Jersey, Virginia and Connecticut agree to indemnify, defend and hold Microdesk harmless from any and all sales tax assessments, fines, penalties, damages and costs including attorney fees incurred as a result of a determination by taxing authorities that the purchase was subject to the payment of sales or use tax.

_____   _____
Authorized Client Signature   Date

_____
Print Name

CANCELLATION POLICY

ATC Classes - Reservations can be modified or cancelled at no charge up to 5 business days prior to the start of the class. If 5 days notice is not provided you will be charged for the full cost of the class, which will be held as a credit to be applied toward another scheduled class held no later than 6 months from the date of cancellation. (Microdesk reserves the right to cancel or reschedule any class based on enrollment)

Custom Training/Services - Scheduled custom training and/or scheduled services may be cancelled by providing written notice 5 business days prior to the scheduled services start or delivery date. If proper notice is not provided we reserve the right to charge for any service to be held within that five 5 day period.

Acknowledgement - Order #F7712205 has been received
4 messages

Fry's Electronics <order_ rmation@i.frys.com>   Thu, Oct 16, 2014 at 7:31 AM

Thank you for ordering from Frys.com!

We are pleased to inform you that your order for the item(s) shown below has been successfully received
Your order number is F7712205 and will be shipped as soon as available.

PLU#	Item Description	Qty	Receive By (est.)	unit price	ext price
8119135	Toshiba C55-B 5298, Intel Celeron N2830, 15.6" Display, Laptop With 4GB Memory, 500GB Hard Drive, Windows 8.1	1	Tuesday, October 21	$227	$227
4102643	California Electronic Waste Recycle Fee > 15 in < 35 Non Taxable	1		$4	$4.0
7091541	Apple 13.3" MacBook Pro dual-core Intel Core i5 2.5GHz, 4GB RAM, 500GB 5400-rpm hard drive, Intel HD Graphics 4000, Ships with Mountain Lion (MD101LL/A)	2	Tuesday, October 21	$1099	$2198
4102503	California Electronic Waste Recycle Fee > 4 in < 15 Non Taxable	2		$3	$6.0
7869919	Apple 21.5" iMac Quad-Core Intel Core i5 2.7GHz (4th generation Haswell processor), 8GB RAM, 1TB Hard Drive, Intel Iris Pro graphics, 2 Thunderbolt ports, 802.11ac Wi-Fi, Apple Wireless Keyboard, Magic Mouse, OS X Mountain Lion (ME086LL/A)	1	Tuesday, October 21	$1299	$1299
4102663	Monitor Fee > 34 in	1		$5	$5.0

If you have any questions regarding your order, please call 1-877-688-7678

Thank you for choosing Frys.com.

Sincerely,

Fry's Electronics Inc.

Sydney, Australia
+612-402730410
[Quoted text hidden]

---

ip01@i.frys.com <ip01@i.frys.com>   Thu, Oct 16, 2014 at 7:36 AM
To: ████████████

Hello again!

I got your order and will show this to my supervisor for furhter processing

will follow up with you as soon as possible

irina

> Hi,
> I had previously emailed my Australian ID. Attached please find the
> order number receipt
> Sincerely
>
> ████████████
> Sydney, Australia
> +612-402730410
>
> --------- Forwarded Message ---------
> Subject: Acknowledgement - Order #F7712205 has been received
> Date: Wed, 15 Oct 2014 16:31:17 -0400 (EDT)
> From: Fry's Electronics <order_confirmation@i.frys.com>
> To:
>
>
>
>
>
> *Thank you for ordering from Frys.com!*
>
> ████████████
>
> We are pleased to inform you that your order for the item(s) shown below
> has been successfully received
> Your order number is F7712205 and will be shipped as soon as available.
>
> PLU#   Item Description   Qty   Receive By (est.)   unit price   ext price
> 8119135   Toshiba C55-B5298, Intel Celeron N2830, 15.6" Display, Laptop
> With 4GB Memory, 500GB Hard Drive, Windows 8.1   1   Tuesday, October 21
> $227 $227
> 4102643   California Electronic Waste Recycle Fee > 15 in < 35 *Non
> Taxable*   1
> $4 $4.0
> 7091541   Apple 13.3" MacBook Pro dual-core Intel Core i5 2.5GHz, 4GB
> RAM, 500GB 5400-rpm hard drive, Intel HD Graphics 4000, Ships with
> Mountain Lion (MD101LL/A)   2   Tuesday, October 21 $1099 $2198
> 4102603   California Electronic Waste Recycle Fee > 4 in < 15 *Non
> Taxable*   2
> $3 $6.0

> 7869919   Apple 21.5" iMac Quad-Core Intel Core i5 2.7GHz (4th generation
> Haswell processor), 8GB RAM, 1TB Hard Drive, Intel Iris Pro graphics, 2
> Thunderbolt ports, 802.11ac Wi-Fi, Apple Wireless Keyboard, Magic Mouse,
> OS X Mountain Lion (ME086LL/A)   1   Tuesday, October 21 $1299 $1299
> 4102663   Monitor Fee > 34 in   1
> $5 $5.0
>
>
>
> If you have any questions regarding your order, please call
> 1-877-688-7678.
>
> Thank you for choosing Frys.com.
>
> Sincerely,
>
> Fry's Electronics Inc.
>
>
>
>

Irina N Paulson
Customer Service Associate
ip01@i.frys.com

---

ip01@i.frys.com <ip01@i.frys.com>   Thu, Oct 16, 2014 at 8:53 AM

looks like everything is processed just fine and its in process of being

shipped out! tracking number will become available once it ships and you

will be able to track this within 24 hours

thanks for your patience

irina

>
> Hi,
> I had previously emailed my Australian ID. Attached please find the
> order number receipt
> Sincerely
>
>
>
> +612-402730410
>
> ------- Forwarded Message -------
> Subject: Acknowledgement - Order #F7712205 has been received
> Date: Wed, 15 Oct 2014 16:31:17 -0400 (EDT)

> From: Fry's Electronics <order_confirmation@i.frys.com>
> To: ███████
>
>
>
>
>
>
> *Thank you for ordering from Frys.com!*
>
> ███████
>
> We are pleased to inform you that your order for the item(s) shown below
> has been successfully received
> Your order number is F7712205 and will be shipped as soon as available.
>
> PLU#   Item Description   Qty   Receive By (est.)   unit price   ext price
> 8119135   Toshiba C55-B5298, Intel Celeron N2830, 15.6" Display, Laptop
> With 4GB Memory, 500GB Hard Drive, Windows 8.1   1   Tuesday, October 21
> $227 $227
> 4102643   California Electronic Waste Recycle Fee > 15 in < 35 *Non
> Taxable *   1
> $4 $4.0
> 7091541   Apple 13.3" MacBook Pro dual-core Intel Core i5 2.5GHz, 4GB
> RAM, 500GB 5400-rpm hard drive, Intel HD Graphics 4000, Ships with
> Mountain Lion (MD101LL/A)   2   Tuesday, October 21 $1099 $2198
> 4102603   California Electronic Waste Recycle Fee > 4 in < 15 *Non
> Taxable *   2
> $3 $6.0
> 7869919   Apple 21.5" iMac Quad-Core Intel Core i5 2.7GHz (4th generation
> Haswell processor), 8GB RAM, 1TB Hard Drive, Intel Iris Pro graphics, 2
> Thunderbolt ports, 802.11ac Wi-Fi, Apple Wireless Keyboard, Magic Mouse,
> OS X Mountain Lion (ME086LL/A)   1   Tuesday, October 21 $1299 $1299
> 4102663   Monitor Fee > 34 in   1
> $5 $5.0
>
>
>
> If you have any questions regarding your order, please call
> 1-877-688-7678.
>
> Thank you for choosing Frys.com.
>
> Sincerely,
>
> Fry's Electronics Inc.
>
>
>
>

[Quoted text hidden]

Transaction history

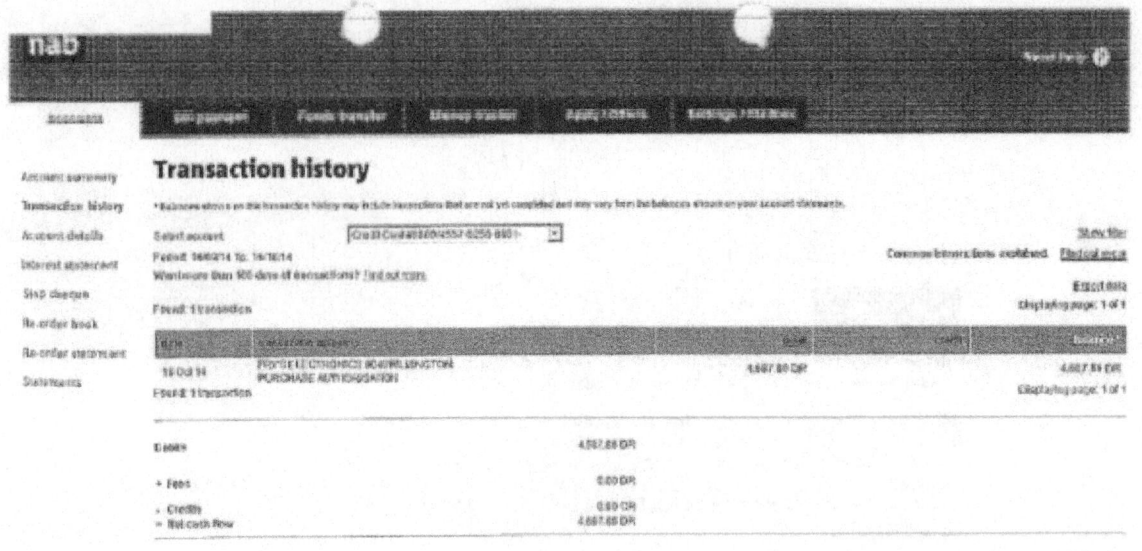

Date	Description	Debit	Credit	Balance
16 Oct 14	JB HI-FI ELECTRONICS #04 WELLINGTON PURCHASE AUTHORISATION	4,687.88 DR		4,687.88 DR

- Debits: 4,687.88 DR
- + Fees: 0.00 DR
- – Credits: 0.00 DR
- = Net cash flow: 4,687.88 DR

Rocscience

#780-439 University Avenue,
Toronto, Ontario M5G 1Y8
CANADA
Tel: (416) 698-8217

Invoice

Date	Invoice #
01/03/2015	9743

BILL TO

███████ Works, Inc.
███████ #3
Los Angeles, CA
USA 90034

SHIP TO

███████ Works, Inc.
███████ #3
Los Angeles, CA
USA 90034

P.O. NO.	TERMS	REP	SHIPPED	VIA	CUSTOMER NO.	CONTACT NAME
	Prepayment	AJS		UPS	18015	

Item	Description	Unit Price	Qty	Amount
SL (6.0)	Slide v6.029 - Windows License No. 8015A	2,495.00	1	2,495.00
	USB 010514, HASP lock Manual available online			
	For Rocscience Use Only Key ID:			
Shipping/Hand	Shipping/Handling Cost	50.00		50.00
Shipping/Hand	Bankwire Transfer Fee* *Fee will be waived if not paying by BWT	25.00		25.00
	Subtotal USD			2,570.00
	Registered to:			
	███████ Works, Inc. Los Angeles, CA, USA			

Total in US Dollars

GST/HST No. ███████

Total USD 2,570.00

PLAXIS

Created Date
Expiration Date
Our Reference
Quote Number

Quote to:

Company: ████████ Works, Inc.
Address: ████████ #3
Los Angeles, CA 90034
U.S.A.

Contact:
Email:
Phone:

Product	Description	Quantity	Sales Price	Total Price
PLAXIS 2D - Standalone First	Optional 2D-Dynamics & 2D-PlaxFlow not Included	1.00	USD 9,000.00	USD 9,000.00
PLAXIS VIP for PLAXIS 2D - First Licence	One year PLAXIS VIP	1.00	USD 1,250.00	USD 1,250.00
Postage and Handling		1.00	USD 100.00	USD 100.00

Subtotal	USD 10,350.00
VAT / TAX %	0.00%
VAT / TAX Amount	USD 0.00
Total	USD 10,350.00

Payment Info

Quote on payment   S04258314

BIC/SWIFT: WFBIUS6S
Wells Fargo Account no.: 855 830 2223
Routing no. 111900659

Plaxis Americas LLC
2500 Wilcrest Drive, Suite 300
Houston, TX 77042

sales@plaxis.nl
www.plaxis.nl

Bentley®
Sustaining Infrastructure

19 November 2014

███████ Works, Inc.
███████ #3
LOS ANGELES CA 90034
USA

███████

███████

Additional Information about our products and the benefits of SELECT can be found at http://www.bentley.com. We look forward to receiving your purchase order and fulfilling our commitment to you, our valued customer!

If I may be of any further assistance, please do not hesitate to call the number below.

Thank you for your interest in Bentley products.

Yours sincerely,

Linda Grubb
+1 (610) 458-5000

Bentley Account Manager

Bentley Systems, Incorporated 685 Stockton Drive, Exton, PA 19341
Phone: 1 800 513 5103   Fax: +1 (610) 458 2779
Website: www.bentley.com   E-mail: bac@bentley.com

PAGE 158

Bentley
Sustaining Infrastructure

Quotation

Quote Number: 40633848
Number of Pages: 2 / 3

Date: 19 November 2014
Valid Until: 19 December 2014
Customer ID: 1004042026

Ship-to: RK Engineering Works, Inc.
▇▇▇▇ #3
LOS ANGELES CA 90034
USA

Bill-to: ▇▇▇▇ Works, Inc.
▇▇▇▇ #3
LOS ANGELES CA 90034
USA

Tel No:
Fax No:

Tel No:
Fax No:

If your organization is a subscriber to Bentley SELECT, the pricing listed on this page of the quote is prorated to the end of your current billing cycle. If applicable, future invoices will be generated based on the billing cycle shown on the following pages. The total from this first section of the quote is your immediate purchase value.

Products/Services

No.	Part # Description	Quantity	Unit Pricing		Total
200	4589/ gINT Logs Perpetual License	1	Gross Value	927.00	927.00
			Net Price	927.00	

Products/Services Sub Total	927.00
Total of Immediate Purchase	927.00
Grand Total of Quote (over life of contract)	927.00
Currency	USD

Prices shown on this quotation are not inclusive of applicable taxes. Applicable taxes will be included on invoices. If your account is exempt from standard taxes, please provide supporting documentation with your order.

Bentley Systems, Incorporated 685 Stockton Drive, Exton, PA 19341
Phone: 1 800 513 5103   Fax: +1 (610) 4582779
Website: www.bentley.com   E-mail: bac@bentley.com

Bentley
Sustaining Infrastructure

Quotation

Quote Number:
Number of Pages:

Export Control:

You acknowledge that these commodities, technology or software are subject to the export control laws, rules, regulations, restrictions and national security controls of the United States and other agencies or authorities based outside of the United States (the "Export Controls").

You must not export, re-export or transfer, whether directly or indirectly, the commodities, technology or software, or any portion thereof, or any system containing such commodities, technology or software or portion thereof, without first complying strictly and fully with all Export Controls that may be imposed on them.

The countries subject to restriction by action of the United States Government or any other governmental agency or authority based outside of the United States, are subject to change, and it is your responsibility to comply with the applicable United States Government requirements, or those of any other governmental agency or authority based outside of the United States, as they may be amended from time to time. For additional information, see http://www.bis.doc.gov

Bentley is subject to the United States Department of the Treasury Office of Foreign Assets Control (OFAC) Sanctions Programs regulations. Those regulations require Bentley not engage in transactions (1) with designated persons and entities set forth on OFAC's Specially Designated Nationals List ("SDN List"), see http://www.treasury.gov/ofac/downloads/ctrylst.txt , or (2) where a customer intends to finance a purchase of Bentley software and/or technology through new debt or equity by or for entities identified on OFAC's Sectoral Sanctions Identifications List ("SSI List"), see http://www.treasury.gov/ofac/downloads/ssi/ssi_ctrylst.txt. Accordingly, Bentley will not engage in such transactions.

**** Note:**

Pricing is only applicable to the products and quantities contained within this quote and may not be applied to a subset of the quotation. If you are a SELECT Subscriber, the terms of your SELECT Program Agreement shall apply to any purchases made pursuant to this quote.

Your payment term shall be: Net 30 Days

Any additional or different terms or conditions appearing on your purchase order, even if Bentley acknowledges such terms and conditions, shall not be binding on the parties unless both parties agree in a separate written agreement.

Agreed and accepted by:

If you would like us to bill this quote against a Purchase Order, please indicate the purchase order number below and attach a copy with your acceptance of this quote.

_____
(Subscriber's Signature)

☐ Please bill against PO N# _____

_____
(Subscriber's Name)

☐ Purchase Order is not required. We will accept Bentley's invoice on the basis of this signed quote.

_____
(Title)

_____
(Subscriber's Signature)

_____
(Date)

_____
(Date)

Bentley Contact:
Name: Linda Grubb
Tel: +1 (610) 458-5000

Bentley Systems, Incorporated 685 Stockton Drive, Exton, PA 19341
Phone: 1 800 513 5103   Fax: +1 (610) 458 2779
Website: www.bentley.com   E-mail: bac@bentley.com

CivilTech Software
sales@civiltech.com
Phone: 888-812-9525
Fax: 425-998-0145

Civiltech Software
18707 SE Newport Way, #406
Issaquah, WA 98027

Quote

Date: 11/17/14

Bill To: [redacted]

Ship To:
Phone:
Fax:
Email: [redacted]

Invoice Number: 41517
PO Number:

Payment Term: Net30

Quantity	DESCRIPTION	UNIT PRICE	TOTAL VALUE
1	LiquefyPro V5 with USB key	$900.00	$900.00
1	Regular US Shipping and Handling		$10.00
		Total Invoiced	$910.00

THANK YOU FOR YOUR BUSINESS!

ENSOFT, INC.

3003 West Howard Lane
Austin, Texas 78728
512-244-6464 fax 512-244-6067

No.: 7459

QUOTE

Company:	RK Engineering Works, Inc.					Date	11/18/2014
Contact:						Shipment	UPS 2 Day
Address:	11131 Rose Avenue #3						
City:	Los Angeles	State:	CA	Zip:	90034	No. of pages	1 of 1
Phone:		Email:		@gmail.com			

Qty	Description	Unit Price	TOTAL
	Software:		
1	GROUP 2014/v9 (single user license) - Includes a USB Key and pdf Manuals	$ 1,800.00	$ 1,800.00
1	LPILE 2013/v7 (single user license) - Includes a USB Key and pdf Manuals	$ 1,000.00	$ 1,000.00
1	SHAFT 2012/v7 (single user license) - Includes a USB Key and pdf Manuals	$ 850.00	$ 850.00
	Yearly Maintenance Fee:		
	Yearly Maintenance Fee for GROUP-1SingleUser (after first year) = $270.00		
	Yearly Maintenance Fee for LPILE-1SingleUser (after first year) = $150.00		
	Yearly Maintenance Fee for SHAFT-1SingleUser (after first year) = $130.00		
	Please note that there is an additional charge for every six months that pass w/out renewal		
	Maintenance Expiration Date: TBD		
	Pricing is subject to change without prior notice.		

Note: Please make sure that all information on this QUOTE is correct. Make any changes necessary at time of ordering. Also, when ordering please include this QUOTE NUMBER along with method of payment. *QUOTE IS ONLY VALID FOR 30 DAYS*

Bill To: same as above

End User/Licensed To: same as above

Payment Details
- ○ Purchase Order
- ○ Wire Transfer
- ● Credit Card _____

Name:
CC:
Exp:
Billing:

SubTotal	$ 3,650.00
Shipping & Handling	$ 20.00
Taxes 8.25%	$ -
TOTAL	**$ 3,670.00**
	USD ONLY

In case of questions please contact Ensoft Sales:
5122446464 (ext 1) or sales@ensoftinc.com

ENSOFT, INC.
Tax ID 974-2354747

Monthly Bank Statements

CHASE ◯

JPMorgan Chase Bank, N.A.
P O Box 659754
San Antonio, TX 78265 - 9754

January 01, 2015 through January 30, 2015

Account Number:

CUSTOMER SERVICE INFORMATION

Web site:	www.Chase.com
Service Center:	1-877-425-8100
Deaf and Hard of Hearing:	1-800-242-7383
Para Espanol:	1-888-6224273
International Calls:	1-713-262-1679

00017621 DRE 703 142 03515 NNNNNNNNNNN T 1 000000000 04 0000

WORKS
1000 MACDONALD AVE APT 120
RICHMOND CA 94801-3151

CHECKING SUMMARY | Chase Performance Business Checking

	INSTANCES	AMOUNT
Beginning Balance		$206.77
Deposits and Additions	1	400.00
ATM & Debit Card Withdrawals	4	- 493.55
Fees and Other Withdrawals	1	- 100.00
Ending Balance	6	$13.22

DEPOSITS AND ADDITIONS

DATE	DESCRIPTION	AMOUNT
01/20	Chase Quickpay Electronic Transfer 4392825856 From Chetankumar H Shah	$400.00
	Total Deposits and Additions	$400.00

ATM & DEBIT CARD WITHDRAWALS

DATE	DESCRIPTION		AMOUNT
01/20	Card Purchase	01/18 Cheapoair.Com Air Cheapoair.Com NY Card 8318	$396.00
01/27	Card Purchase Taka	01/26 Pan Pacific Sonargaon Dhaka Card 8318	5.82
	440.00 X 0.01286364 (Exchg Rte) + 0.16 (Exchg Rte ADJ)		
01/27	Card Purchase Taka	01/26 Baburchi Jigatala Tso Card 8318	7.53
	569.25 X 0.01285903 (Exchg Rte) + 0.21 (Exchg Rte ADJ)		
01/28	Card Purchase Taka	01/26 Pan Pacific Sonargaon Dhaka Card 8318	84.20
	6349.98 X 0.01287406 (Exchg Rte) + 2.45 (Exchg Rte ADJ)		
	Total ATM & Debit Card Withdrawals		$493.55

ATM & DEBIT CARD SUMMARY

CHASE

January 01, 2015 through January 30, 2015
Account Number: 000000629593653

Rafel Zafar Card 8318

Total ATM Withdrawals & Debits	$0.00
Total Card Purchases	$493.55
Total Card Deposits & Credits	$0.00

ATM & Debit Card Totals

Total ATM Withdrawals & Debits	$0.00
Total Card Purchases	$493.55
Total Card Deposits & Credits	$0.00

FEES AND OTHER WITHDRAWALS

DATE	DESCRIPTION	AMOUNT
01/06	Service Charges For The Month of December	$100.00
	Total Fees & Other Withdrawals	$100.00

You were charged a monthly service fee of $20.00 this period. You can avoid this fee in the future by maintaining a relationship balance (combined business deposits) of $50,000.00. Your relationship balance was $120.00.

DAILY ENDING BALANCE

DATE	AMOUNT
01/06	$106.77
01/20	110.77
01/27	97.42
01/28	13.22

SERVICE CHARGE SUMMARY

Maintenance Fee	$20.00
Excess Product Fees	$0.00
Other Service Charges	$0.00
Total Service Charges	$20.00 Will be assessed on 2/4/15

TRANSACTIONS FOR SERVICE FEE CALCULATION	NUMBER OF TRANSACTIONS
Checks Paid / Debits	4
Deposits / Credits	0
Deposited Items	0
Total Transactions	4

Chase Performance Business Checking allows up to 350 checks, deposits, and deposited items per statement cycle. Your transaction total for this cycle was 4.

CHASE

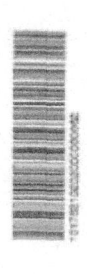

January 01, 2015 through January 30, 2015
Account Number:

SERVICE CHARGE DETAIL

DESCRIPTION Your Product Includes:	VOLUME	ALLOWED	CHARGED	PRICE/UNIT	TOTAL
ACCOUNT 000000625593653					
Monthly Service Fee	1			$20.00	$20.00
Transactions	4	350	0	$0.00	$0.00
Total Service Charge (Will be assessed on 2/4/15)					$20.00
ACCOUNT 000000629593653					
Monthly Service Fee	1				
Transactions	4				

CHASE

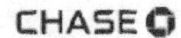

January 01, 2015 through January 30, 2015
Account Number:

BALANCING YOUR CHECKBOOK

Note: Ensure your checkbook register is up to date with all transactions to date whether they are included on your statement or not.

1. Write in the Ending Balance shown on this statement: Step 1 Balance: $ _____

2. List and total all deposits & additions not shown on this statement:

Date	Amount	Date	Amount	Date	Amount

Step 2 Total: $ _____

3. Add Step 2 Total to Step 1 Balance.   Step 3 Total: $ _____

4. List and total all checks, ATM withdrawals, debit card purchases and other withdrawals not shown on this statement.

Check Number or Date	Amount	Check Number or Date	Amount

Step 4 Total: -$ _____

5. Subtract Step 4 Total from Step 3 Total. This should match your Checkbook Balance: $ _____

IN CASE OF ERRORS OR QUESTIONS ABOUT YOUR ELECTRONIC FUNDS TRANSFERS:Call or write us at the phone number or address on the front of this statement (non-personal accounts contact Customer Service) if you think your statement or receipt is incorrect or if you need more information about a transfer listed on the statement or receipt. We must hear from you no later than 60 days after we sent you the FIRST statement on which the problem or error appeared. Be prepared to give us the following information:
- Your name and account number
- The dollar amount of the suspected error
- A description of the error or transfer you are unsure of, why you believe it is an error, or why you need more information.

We will investigate your complaint and will correct any error promptly. If we take more than 10 business days (or 20 business days for new accounts) to do this, we will credit your account for the amount you think is in error so that you will have use of the money during the time it takes us to complete our investigation.

IN CASE OF ERRORS OR QUESTIONS ABOUT NON-ELECTRONIC TRANSACTIONS:Contact the bank immediately if your statement is incorrect or if you need more information about any non-electronic transactions (checks or deposits) on this statement. If any such error appears, you must notify the bank in writing no later than 30 days after the statement was made available to you. For more complete details, see the Account Rules and Regulations or other applicable account agreement that governs your account.

JPMorgan Chase Bank, N.A. Member FDIC

CHASE ⬡

JPMorgan Chase Bank, N.A.
P O Box 659754
San Antonio, TX 78265-9754

January 31, 2015 through February 27, 2015

Account Number:

CUSTOMER SERVICE INFORMATION

Web site:	Chase.com
Service Center:	1-800-242-7338
Deaf and Hard of Hearing:	1-800-242-7383
Para Espanol:	1-888-622-4273
International Calls:	1-713-262-1679

00018695 DRE 703 142 06315 NNNNNNNNNNN T 1 000000060 D4 0000

WORKS
1000 MACDONALD AVE APT 120
RICHMOND CA 94801-3151

We are updating your Deposit Account Agreement

We will update the Electronic Funds Transfer Service Terms in your agreement for business accounts effective March 22, 2015, to cover how you can use an eATM (formerly known as Express Banking kiosk) located inside a branch lobby during the branch operating hours:

- Each signer can withdraw up to $3,000 each day. Business Associate card limits remain the same.
- At certain Chase eATMs, you or an authorized signer will be able to provide us personal identification that we accept, such as a driver's license. Our branch employee will then give you a temporary, one-time code so you can have full use of the eATM.
- All other withdrawals at eATMs count towards your daily ATM withdrawal limit.

These changes will happen over several months, so you should ask an employee in your branch if the eATM has been updated with these changes.

For a copy of your agreement, you can view it anytime by logging in at chase.com and clicking Legal Agreements and Disclosures at the bottom of any page, or visit a branch. If you have questions, please call us at the telephone number listed on this statement.

CHECKING SUMMARY | Chase Performance Business Checking

	INSTANCES	AMOUNT
Beginning Balance		$13.22
Deposits and Additions	1	120.00
ATM & Debit Card Withdrawals	2	- 108.24
Fees and Other Withdrawals	1	- 20.00
Ending Balance	4	$4.98

DEPOSITS AND ADDITIONS

DATE	DESCRIPTION		AMOUNT
02/05	ATM Cash Deposit	02/05 12121 San Pablo Ave Richmond CA Card 8318	$120.00
Total Deposits and Additions			**$120.00**

Page 1 of 4

CHASE

January 31, 2015 through February 27, 2015
Account Number:

ATM & DEBIT CARD WITHDRAWALS

DATE	DESCRIPTION		AMOUNT
02/06	Card Purchase	02/05 Progressive *Insuranc 800-776-4737 OH Card 8318	$93.24
02/13	Card Purchase	02/11 Valero 7528 Mountain View CA Card 8318	15.00
Total ATM & Debit Card Withdrawals			**$108.24**

ATM & DEBIT CARD SUMMARY

Rafel Zafar Card 8318

Total ATM Withdrawals & Debits	$0.00
Total Card Purchases	$108.24
Total Card Deposits & Credits	$120.00

ATM & Debit Card Totals

Total ATM Withdrawals & Debits	$0.00
Total Card Purchases	$108.24
Total Card Deposits & Credits	$120.00

FEES AND OTHER WITHDRAWALS

DATE	DESCRIPTION	AMOUNT
02/04	Service Charges For The Month of January	$20.00
Total Fees & Other Withdrawals		**$20.00**

You were charged a monthly service fee of $20.00 this period. You can avoid this fee in the future by maintaining a relationship balance (combined business deposits) of $50,000.00. Your relationship balance was $12.00.

DAILY ENDING BALANCE

DATE	AMOUNT
02/04	-$6.78
02/05	113.22
02/06	19.98
02/13	4.98

SERVICE CHARGE SUMMARY

Maintenance Fee	$20.00
Excess Product Fees	$0.00
Other Service Charges	$0.00
Total Service Charges	**$20.00** Will be assessed on 3/4/15

CHASE

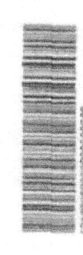

January 31, 2015 through February 27, 2015

Account Number:

SERVICE CHARGE SUMMARY (continued)

TRANSACTIONS FOR SERVICE FEE CALCULATION	NUMBER OF TRANSACTIONS
Checks Paid / Debits	2
Deposits / Credits	0
Deposited Items	1
Total Transactions	**3**

Chase Performance Business Checking allows up to 350 checks, deposits, and deposited items per statement cycle. Your transaction total for this cycle was 3.

SERVICE CHARGE DETAIL

DESCRIPTION Your Product Includes:	VOLUME	ALLOWED	CHARGED	PRICE/ UNIT	TOTAL
ACCOUNT 000000629593653					
Monthly Service Fee	1			$20.00	$20.00
Transactions	3	350	0	$0.00	$0.00
Total Service Charge (Will be assessed on 3/4/15)					$20.00
ACCOUNT 000000629593653					
Monthly Service Fee	1				
Transactions	3				

CHASE

January 31, 2015 through February 27, 2015
Account Number:

BALANCING YOUR CHECKBOOK

Note: Ensure your checkbook register is up to date with all transactions to date whether they are included on your statement or not.

1. Write in the Ending Balance shown on this statement: Step 1 Balance: $_____

2. List and total all deposits & additions not shown on this statement:

Date	Amount	Date	Amount	Date	Amount

Step 2 Total: $_____

3. Add Step 2 Total to Step 1 Balance.   Step 3 Total: $_____

4. List and total all checks, ATM withdrawals, debit card purchases and other withdrawals not shown on this statement.

Check Number or Date	Amount	Check Number or Date	Amount

Step 4 Total: -$_____

5. Subtract Step 4 Total from Step 3 Total. This should match your Checkbook Balance: $_____

IN CASE OF ERRORS OR QUESTIONS ABOUT YOUR ELECTRONIC FUNDS TRANSFERS:Call or write us at the phone number or address on the front of this statement (non-personal accounts contact Customer Service) if you think your statement or receipt is incorrect or if you need more information about a transfer listed on the statement or receipt. We must hear from you no later than 60 days after we sent you the FIRST statement on which the problem or error appeared. Be prepared to give us the following information:
- Your name and account number
- The dollar amount of the suspected error
- A description of the error or transfer you are unsure of, why you believe it is an error, or why you need more information.

We will investigate your complaint and will correct any error promptly. If we take more than 10 business days (or 20 business days for new accounts) to do this, we will credit your account for the amount you think is in error so that you will have use of the money during the time it takes us to complete our investigation.

IN CASE OF ERRORS OR QUESTIONS ABOUT NON-ELECTRONIC TRANSACTIONS:Contact the bank immediately if your statement is incorrect or if you need more information about any non-electronic transactions (checks or deposits) on this statement. If any such error appears, you must notify the bank in writing no later than 30 days after the statement was made available to you. For more complete details, see the Account Rules and Regulations or other applicable account agreement that governs your account.

JPMorgan Chase Bank, N.A. Member FDIC

CHASE

JPMorgan Chase Bank, N.A.
P O Box 659754
San Antonio, TX 78265-9754

00617992 DRE 703 142 09316 NNNNNNNNNN T 1000000000 04 0000

███████ WORKS
1000 MACDONALD AVE APT 120
RICHMOND CA 94801-3151

CUSTOMER SERVICE INFORMATION

Web site:	Chase.com
Service Center:	1-800-242-7338
Deaf and Hard of Hearing:	1-800-242-7383
Para Espanol:	1-888-622-4273
International Calls:	1-713-262-1679

CHECKING SUMMARY
Chase Performance Business Checking

	INSTANCES	AMOUNT
Beginning Balance		$4.98
Deposits and Additions	2	30,061.57
Checks Paid	1	-1,700.00
ATM & Debit Card Withdrawals	7	-1,434.64
Electronic Withdrawals	1	-23,500.00
Fees and Other Withdrawals	3	-730.00
Ending Balance	14	$2,701.91

DEPOSITS AND ADDITIONS

DATE	DESCRIPTION	AMOUNT
03/05	Fedwire Credit Via: The Bank of New York Mellon/021000018 B/O: ███████ Works Inc Nsw 2064 Australia Ref: Chase Nyc/Ctr/Bnf=███████ Works Richmond, CA 948013151/Ac-00000 0006295 Rfb=3E9Da880 Obi=Transfer FROM Australia For Escrow Imad: 0305B1Q8153C003147 Tm: 2085609064Ff	$25,061.57
03/13	Mahabub Alam Sender ███████ CIE ID: T941687665	5,000.00
Total Deposits and Additions		**$30,061.57**

CHECKS PAID

CHECK NO.	DESCRIPTION	DATE PAID	AMOUNT
1032 ^		03/31	$1,700.00
Total Checks Paid			**$1,700.00**

If you see a description in the Checks Paid section, it means that we received only electronic information about the check, not the original or an image of the check. As a result, we're not able to return the check to you or show you an image.

^ An image of this check may be available for you to view on Chase.com.

CHASE

February 26, 2015 through March 31, 2015
Account Number:

ATM & DEBIT CARD WITHDRAWALS

DATE	DESCRIPTION		AMOUNT
03/09	ATM Withdrawal	03/09 12121 San Pablo Ave Richmond CA Card 8318	$140.00
03/12	ATM Withdrawal	03/12 12121 San Pablo Ave Richmond CA Card 8318	400.00
03/17	ATM Withdrawal	03/17 12121 San Pablo Ave Richmond CA Card 8318	360.00
03/20	Card Purchase	03/18 AT&T S10M 10723 Richmond CA Card 8318	70.85
03/25	ATM Withdrawal	03/25 2230 Barrett Ave Richmond CA Card 8318	60.00
03/26	Card Purchase	03/25 Usps 05646201133509167 Richmond CA Card 8318	3.79
03/31	ATM Withdrawal	03/31 2230 Barrett Ave Richmond CA Card 8318	400.00
Total ATM & Debit Card Withdrawals			**$1,434.64**

ATM & DEBIT CARD SUMMARY

Rafel Zafar Card 8318

	Total ATM Withdrawals & Debits	$1,360.00
	Total Card Purchases	$74.64
	Total Card Deposits & Credits	$0.00

ATM & Debit Card Totals

	Total ATM Withdrawals & Debits	$1,360.00
	Total Card Purchases	$74.64
	Total Card Deposits & Credits	$0.00

ELECTRONIC WITHDRAWALS

DATE	DESCRIPTION	AMOUNT
03/18	03/18 Online Wire Transfer Via: Uniti Bk Buena Pk/122243415 A/C: Tower Escrow Inc. Los Angeles CA 90010 US Imad: 0318B1Qgc07C005223 Trn: 3372500077Es	$23,500.00
Total Electronic Withdrawals		**$23,500.00**

FEES AND OTHER WITHDRAWALS

DATE	DESCRIPTION	AMOUNT
03/04	Service Charges For The Month of February	$20.00
03/11	03/11 Withdrawal	500.00
03/26	03/26 Withdrawal	210.00
Total Fees & Other Withdrawals		**$730.00**

You were charged a monthly service fee of $20.00 this period. You can avoid this fee in the future by maintaining a relationship balance (combined business deposits) of $50,000.00. Your relationship balance was $12,742.00.

CHASE

February 28, 2015 through March 31, 2015
Account Number:

DAILY ENDING BALANCE

DATE	AMOUNT	DATE	AMOUNT
03/04	-$15.02	03/17	28,646.55
03/05	25,046.55	03/18	5,146.55
03/09	24,906.55	03/20	5,075.70
03/11	24,406.55	03/25	5,015.70
03/12	24,006.55	03/26	4,801.91
03/13	29,006.55	03/31	2,701.91

SERVICE CHARGE SUMMARY

Maintenance Fee	$20.00
Excess Product Fees	$0.00
Other Service Charges	$0.00
Total Service Charges	**$20.00** Will be assessed on 4/3/15

TRANSACTIONS FOR SERVICE FEE CALCULATION	NUMBER OF TRANSACTIONS
Checks Paid / Debits	11
Deposits / Credits	2
Deposited Items	0
Total Transactions	**13**

Chase Performance Business Checking allows up to 350 checks, deposits, and deposited items per statement cycle. Your transaction total for this cycle was 13.

SERVICE CHARGE DETAIL

DESCRIPTION
Your Product Includes:

	VOLUME	ALLOWED	CHARGED	PRICE/UNIT	TOTAL
ACCOUNT					
Monthly Service Fee	1			$20.00	$20.00
Transactions	13	350	0	$0.00	$0.00
Outgoing Wire - Domestic Online	1	1	0	$25.00	$0.00
Subtotal					$20.00
Other Fees					
Incoming Wires - Domestic	1	1	0	$15.00	$0.00
Total Service Charge (Will be assessed on 4/3/15)					$20.00
ACCOUNT					
Monthly Service Fee	1				
Transactions	13				
Outgoing Wire - Domestic Online	1				
Incoming Wires - Domestic	1				

CHASE ◯

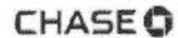

February 28, 2015 through March 31, 2015
Account Number:

BALANCING YOUR CHECKBOOK

Note: Ensure your checkbook register is up to date with all transactions to date whether they are included on your statement or not.

1. Write in the Ending Balance shown on this statement: Step 1 Balance: $ _____

2. List and total all deposits & additions not shown on this statement:

Date	Amount	Date	Amount	Date	Amount

Step 2 Total: $ _____

3. Add Step 2 Total to Step 1 Balance. Step 3 Total: $ _____

4. List and total all checks, ATM withdrawals, debit card purchases and other withdrawals not shown on this statement.

Check Number or Date	Amount	Check Number or Date	Amount

Step 4 Total: -$ _____

5. Subtract Step 4 Total from Step 3 Total. This should match your Checkbook Balance: $ _____

IN CASE OF ERRORS OR QUESTIONS ABOUT YOUR ELECTRONIC FUNDS TRANSFERS: Call or write us at the phone number or address on the front of this statement (non-personal accounts contact Customer Service) if you think your statement or receipt is incorrect or if you need more information about a transfer listed on the statement or receipt. We must hear from you no later than 60 days after we sent you the FIRST statement on which the problem or error appeared. Be prepared to give us the following information:
- Your name and account number
- The dollar amount of the suspected error
- A description of the error or transfer you are unsure of, why you believe it is an error, or why you need more information.

We will investigate your complaint and will correct any error promptly. If we take more than 10 business days (or 20 business days for new accounts) to do this, we will credit your account for the amount you think is in error so that you will have use of the money during the time it takes us to complete our investigation.

IN CASE OF ERRORS OR QUESTIONS ABOUT NON-ELECTRONIC TRANSACTIONS: Contact the bank immediately if your statement is incorrect or if you need more information about any non-electronic transactions (checks or deposits) on this statement. If any such error appears, you must notify the bank in writing no later than 30 days after the statement was made available to you. For more complete details, see the Account Rules and Regulations or other applicable account agreement that governs your account.

JPMorgan Chase Bank, N.A. Member FDIC

Section 4

Business Plan

Business Plan

Business Plan
Prepared May 2015

Contact Information

Table of Contents

Executive Summary 1
    Who We Are 1
    What We Sell 1
    Who We Sell To 5
    Financial Summary 6
Company 7
    Company Overview 7
    Management Team 8
Products and Services 9
    Products and Services 9
    Competitors 10
Target Market 12
    Market Overview 12
    Market Needs 12
Strategy and Implementation 14
    Marketing Plan 14

    Milestones 16
Financial Plan 17
    Revenue Forecast 17
    Personnel Plan 18
    Budget 19
    Profit and Loss Statement 21
Appendix 24
    Revenue Forecast 24
    Personnel Plan 25
    Budget 27
    Profit and Loss Statement 29

Executive Summary

Who We Are

████████ Works provides geo-technical and geo-structural engineering services to Contractors, Architects, Developers, Private property owners and other engineering consultants in the State of California. Mr. ████ is a senior civil engineer with 15 years of experience in geo-technical, geo-structural, and environmental engineering in the United States and Australia.

Mr. ████ has a Bachelors degree in Civil Engineering from California State University, Long Beach and is licensed as a professional engineer (P.E.) in California. With construction activity picking up significantly in California and adjoining states, we expect a strong market for a new geo-technical & geo-structural consultancy. Recent discussion undertaken as part of a market research also confirmed the same. We also feel confident about the success of the firm, as an established engineering consultancy in California has expressed strong interest in obtaining services of RK Engineering Works as soon as it is set up. This relationship will generate immediate cash flow and allow expansion of the consultancy in other service areas within a short period of time.

With a strong marketing strategy and putting to use Mr. ████ extensive knowledge of the California engineering market, we are convinced that the consultancy will likely gross US$400,000.00 and employ 4-5 full time engineers, engineering technicians and office support people within 5 years of formation.

What We Sell

1. GEO-TECHNICAL ENGINEERING

a. Geo-technical and geological site investigation

Geo-technical investigation is performed to obtain ground condition information and interpretation of ground models for engineering analysis.

i. Drilled boreholes with hollow stem augers

ii. Standard Penetration Testing (SPT)

iii. Cone Penetration Testing (CPT)

iv. Dynamic cone Penetration Testing (DCP)

v. Trenches

vi. Pits and deep holes

vii. Push and disturbed bulk samples.

b. Geo-technical Analysis

Geo-technical engineering analysis is performed to determine response of structures such as foundations, piles, walls and their interaction with soil and rock.

i. Slope Stability Analysis (SLOPEW/ or SLIDE).

ii. Pile Capacity Analysis (LPILE, GROUP).

iii. Retaining Structures (WALLAP, CT-SHORING, PLAXIS, other in-house software).

iv. Earthquake effects (liquefaction).

v. Site Specific Earthquake Assessment and potential effects on proposed structures.

c. Geo-technical Design Reports

Geo-technical reports are prepared to summarize site investigation data, geo-technical analysis, and engineering recommendations for proposed structure(s).

d. Geo-technical Site Inspections during construction

Site inspection by the geo-technical engineer (or representative) is required by authorities to ensure construction is being undertaken in accordance with plans. Inspection forms and reports are to be provided for records and submission to appropriate authorities.

2. GEO-STRUCTURAL ENGINEERING

a. Geo-technical Analysis

b. Structural Analysis

Structural Design of various structural elements

i. Soil Nails.

ii. Ground Anchors.

iii. Micropiles.

iv. Support elements such as struts, walers and rakers.

v. Site Specific Earthquake Assessment and potential effects on proposed structures.

vi. Temporary shoring of deep excavations.

vii. Piles and caissons.

c. Construction drawings and reports preparation

i. CAD Works.

d. Site inspection services

i. Ground Anchor Capacity Testing and Acceptance.

ii. Soil Nail Capacity Testing and Acceptance.

iii. Pile and micropile compressive and tensile testing and acceptance.

Geo-technical and geo-structural engineering are considered core services of our firm and we will be able to provide the full spectrum of these services within first year of setting up the consultancy.

We envisage that we will be expanding into materials testing services in the middle of second year or at the beginning of the third year of operation. Materials testing services that we plan to provide are listed below.

3. MATERIALS TESTING

i. Soil moisture content.

ii. Soil particle size distribution.

iii. Soil hydrometer test.

iv. Soil Atterberg limits test.

v. Soil direct Shear Test.

vi. Soil triaxial shear test.

vii. Soil consolidation test.

viii. Soi maximum density-optimum moisture content test.

ix. Concrete compressive and tensile strength testing.

We plan to expand into environmental site assessments and re-mediation design at the fifth year of operation. Environmental site assessment (ESA) reports are usually required during property purchase or planned construction with known environmental contamination issues.

4. ENVIRONMENTAL ENGINEERING

a. Phase I Site Assessments (Phase I ESA)

i. Undertake ownership and usage history research.

ii. Undertake interviews of individuals with information about previous

iii. Prepare Phase I ESA report in accordance with ASTM standards with

b. Phase II Site Assessments (Phase II ESA)

i. Undertake environmental site investigation, soil and water

ii. Submission of soil and water samples for testing.

iii. Prepare ESA phase II report with recommendations of mitigating site usage.recommendations about potential site contamination.sampling.site contamination.

Who We Sell To

Our services are in great demand from:

1) Contractors

2) Developers

3) Architects

4) Other Consultants

5) Private Owners

6) Government projects

Financial Summary

Financial Highlights

The financial plan of the business requires growth financed by positive cash flows from operations. Additional outside investment or owner investment is necessary at the beginning, that we envisage will be paid back in a short span of time from the start of operations.

The new business line is not capital-intensive, but will increase fixed costs of the business which must be covered almost immediately by additional revenues. This is feasible because it is expected that at least one major ready client will use our services without hesitation as they are ready to start using our services once we commence operations.

Financial Highlights by Year

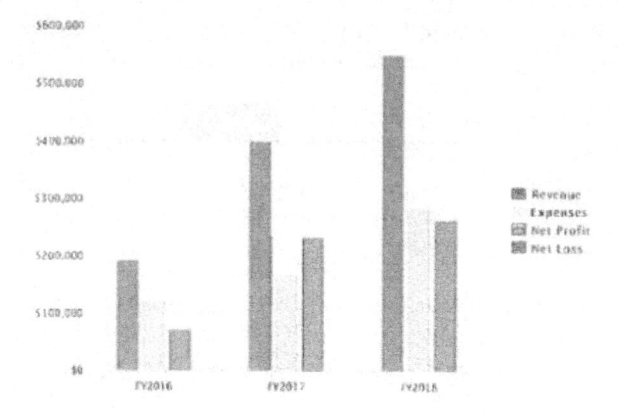

Company

Company Overview

The Civil Engineering Consultancy business will be owned by ▇▇▇▇ M.ASCE. ▇▇▇▇ holds a Civil Engineering degree (BSCE) from California State University Long Beach and has 15 years of civil engineering experience specializing in geo-technical and geo-structural engineering projects.

RK Engineering Works will be incorporated in the State of California for the operation of the engineering consultancy. Other licensing requirements for the operation of the enterprise within City of Los Angeles and for taxation will also be obtained.

Further, ▇▇▇▇ is a licensed Professional Engineer in the State of California and is currently in good standing. ▇▇▇▇ was awarded the "Professional Engineer" (P.E.) designation by California Board of Professional Engineers and Land Surveyors in 2006 after passing testing and fulfilling other requirements. (http://www.bpelsg.ca.gov/consumers/lic_lookup.shtml).

This is a significant achievement, as it will allow ▇▇▇▇ to practice in California as a professional engineer (P.E.) and also makes him eligible to obtain license in many other states in the US. Without a license, engineers cannot approve construction plans and engineering reports in the USA, and without approval by a licensed engineer, plans & reports cannot be used for construction.

▇▇▇▇ is also a member of American Society of Civil Engineers –ASCE (www.asce.org). The American Society of Civil Engineers (ASCE) is America's oldest national engineering society and is the supreme body for civil engineering professionals in America.

▇▇▇▇ brings with him an engineering experience of 10 years in California & 5 years in Australia. He has been part of some high profile projects in both countries and has learnt valuable management skills by leading engineering teams and gained experience in advance engineering methods such as finite element analysis and ground improvement design. ████████ lso has extensive knowledge of many geo-technical and geo-structural engineering and computer aided drafting software.

Currently, ████████ is employed as a geo-technical engineer for a government agency of New South Wales government, Australia.

Management Team

The management team will consist of ████████ for the initial year or two. Following that, ████████ will focus on business development and principal consultancy thereby requiring to employ a team of experienced engineers and technicians to overlook the operations management.

As the Principal Engineer, ████████ will oversee all the Engineering, Marketing and Financial aspects of the firm, with the Engineering and Finance parts being his strong areas of expertise.

The firm will employ an experienced, reliant and dedicated employee to possibly head the operations as well as to carry out marketing activities. The ideal person would be an engineer in the similar field but with an inclination towards the business development side.

The time frame for hiring to this position would be from the midst of the second year of operations as we look to scale up the operations gradually from the very beginning. This also ties in with the fact of being able to groom an experienced and reliable person with whom a strong working understanding can be built within a short span of time.

Products and Services

Products and Services

- Geotechnical and Geo-structural Engineering

This service is performed to performed to obtain ground condition information and interpretation of ground models for engineering analysis as well as to determine response of structures such as foundations, piles, walls and their interaction with soil and rock.

Site inspection by the geo-structural engineer (or representative) is required by authorities to ensure construction is being undertaken in accordance with plans. Inspection forms and reports are to be provided for records and submission to appropriate authorities.

Geotechnical and geo-structural engineering are considered core services of our firm and we will be able to provide the full spectrum of these services within first year of setting up the consultancy.

- Testing for soil, rock and concrete.

We envisage that we will be expanding into materials testing services in the middle of second year or at the beginning of the third year of operation. Materials testing services that we plan to provide are numerous, such as:

Soil moisture content, Soil hydrometer test, Soil direct Shear Test, etc. and the various other tests that are critical for soil analysis.

- Services to Contractors. Developers

We will be providing our services to other reputed firms that are involved in the construction of structures, both large and small. These include developers, architects, contractors, etc.

We will be coordinating with fellow consultants and working out the best possible solution for the problem at hand for any individual project.

Competitors

Our potential competitors are primarily other consultancy firms, both large and small.

Examples of these are:

- AECOM
- Mazetti
- Other regional / local consultancy players in the market
- Conractors

They are considered our competitors as:

1) They are large in size and have a ready presence

2) Their established brand image in the market

3) Large netowrk

However, we are confident that we can do equally well or better than them as for the following facts:

1) We are nimble and hence can address to the customers requirements at a more personal level.

2) We are a professional organisation that can handle both large and small projects. With larger firms, this is difficult as they have a certain minimum amount of project to handle their expenses.

3) We have the engineering services as well as the testing services in-house and therefore can give a discounted rate to clients so as to ensure we get a considerable advantage in our pricing structure.

4) We will ensure that we tie up with contractors so that they will route all their test and consultancy requirements through us thereby leaving their time freed-up to work on the contracting and construction of the project.

Target Market

Market Overview

Market penetration is sometimes referred to as market share. We will penetrate the market by promoting our services to our core customers, which are the contractors, architects, structural engineers and private developers. We will make cold calls, attend various industry gatherings with marketing material, send marketing literature to clients regularly, and employ pricing promotions.

We will focus on what we do best, i.e. geotechnical and geo-structural engineering, and emphasize our services in the market that we will serve. The so called 'concentrated growth strategy' has been selected so that we can concentrate on thoroughly developing and exploiting our knowledge in these areas, and horizontally grow our business by providing services to increased number of clients.

Our core services will be same; we will grow by gaining trust and recognition in the industry. We will also augment our core services by establishing materials testing services, which will result in a varied yet integrated product and increase gross sales.

Finally, once we have grown the business to a level when we can sustain an environmental engineering team, we will grow our service offerings.

Market Needs

Customer needs (herein referred to architects, contractors and other similar consultancies) across the segments are similar in the sense that each seeks high quality, responsive and accurate structural and geo-technical details that will help add value to the structure under construction.

The projects could be of any type, from a small residence to a multi unit dwelling unit to a large corporate office to a dam. In any case, the professionalism and efficiency with which we can provide the information will help sell our professionalism and effectiveness.

Builders, contractors and architectural firms require geo-technical firms who can be nimble and provide alterations to designs as the design grows in form and structure and considering our structure, we will be well placed to offer them this huge advantage.

Especially so since the California market is now in the threshold of a pick up in the construction industry, considering the market meltdown over the last 4-6 years. Finally, as we grow in stature and size, we can add on additional premiums to leverage our brand identity through perceived product uniqueness.

We feel we are in the right market at the right time and our expertise, professionalism and previous working history with California will put us in good stead to develop our practice.

Strategy and Implementation

Marketing Plan

Overview

The major methods of marketing that we will utilize are:

1. Digital target Advertising

2. Personal reviews and network

3. Direct marketing

4. Sales promotion through intermediaries &/or direct

5. Public Relations with suppliers, peers, other consultants

6. Sponsorship of community based events

7. Active participation in association meetings and presenting papers / lectures

Positioning

We're a geo-technical engineering service corporation who leaves no stone unturned to give the best solution to the client.

Pricing

The present pricing structure for this type of consultancy is based on the project cost and timelines of the projects.

We will start off with providing a discount of between 50% to 100% on the material testing reports (depending on the size of the project) if the client also provides us with the agreement to provide them consultancy services.

Also, we will look into the possibility of providing referral discounts to clients who are referred to clients from another one of our clients. This way we will be looking at a chain reaction and possibility increase in business.

Promotion

Promotion will be initially spearheaded by public relations because of its low cost and targeted audience. This would follow through advertising once the practice begins to increase cash flow to an acceptable figure.

Distribution

At the present time, we will only have one level, max two, between ourselves and the consumer. In most cases this will be the other consultants / contractors / developer.

We may look at selling directly to the consumer via online target marketing and specialised magazines, but this will need further study to analyse its impact.

Milestones

Milestone	Due Date
Purchase company vehicle	March 27, 2015
Finalise Office Space	April 13, 2015
Entered into escrow	April 17, 2015
Visa application complete	May 29, 2015
Marketing activity commences	June 29, 2015
Travel over to USA	July 01, 2015
First Project Bagged	September 14, 2015
Recruitment of staff commences	August 01, 2016
Recruitment of Office Manager Completed	September 02, 2016
2 New Staff Join Firm	April 03, 2017

Financial Plan

Revenue Forecast

Revenue Forecast

	FY2016	FY2017	FY2018
Total Revenue	$192,000	$400,000	$550,000
Total Direct Cost	$3,840	$8,000	$11,000
Gross Margin	$188,160	$392,000	$539,000
Gross Margin %	98%	98%	98%

Revenue by Month

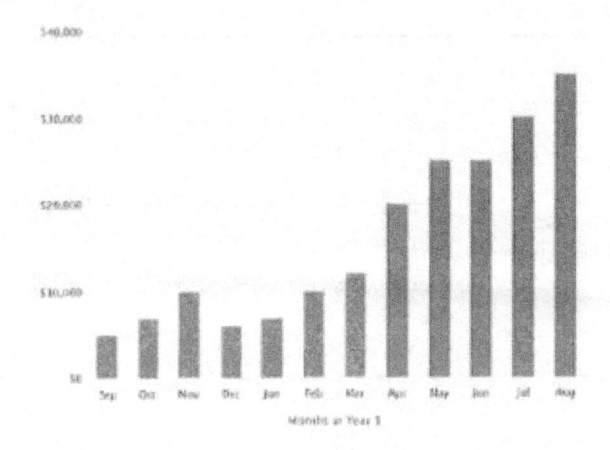

About the Revenue Forecast

The sales projections start in the month of September 2015. Sales steadily increase along with the awareness of our firm through the next 4 months. In December, there is a small dip in consultancy due to the holiday period and then a steady rise through the months of February 2016 onwards. There is a traditional slow season that runs through November and December each year.

Our consultancy charges are estimated to be 1% to 10% of the total project cost, depending on the scope of work, scale of work and timelines. The gross margin will range from 35% to 45%. There is a 25% growth predicted for the second year of sales driven by awareness, growth in market penetration and growth in sales.

The immediate goal is to achieve robust sales in the first year. It is thought that double digit percentage total sales increases can be achieved and maintained throughout the five years of this business plan.

Personnel Plan

Personnel Table

	FY2016	FY2017	FY2018
Director	$48,000	$50,400	$52,920
Operations Manager	$0	$36,000	$37,800
Geotechnical Engineer	$0	$0	$25,000
Geotechnical Technician	$0	$0	$20,000
Engineering Technologist	$0	$0	$28,000
CAD Drafter	$0	$0	$18,000
Total	$48,000	$86,400	$181,720

About the Personnel Plan

The personnel forecast reflects modest raises for all staff each year. The Director will be primarily compensated through profits. It is expected that lower-level staff may turn over, but the positions will be systematized to an extent that this does not disrupt the business.

Budget

Budget Table

	FY2016	FY2017	FY2018
Operating Expenses			
Salary	$48,000	$86,400	$181,720
Employee Related Expenses	$4,800	$8,640	$18,172
Marketing & Promotions	$3,500	$3,000	$4,000
Rent	$3,000	$4,000	$5,000
Utilities	$1,800	$2,200	$2,800
Office Supplies	$3,600	$4,000	$4,500
Insurance	$12,000	$13,500	$15,000
Conveyance	$6,000	$7,200	$8,400
Office Maintenance	$4,595	$5,000	$5,500
Equipment Purchase	$21,200	$0	$0
Total Operating Expenses	**$108,495**	**$133,940**	**$245,092**

Expenses by Month

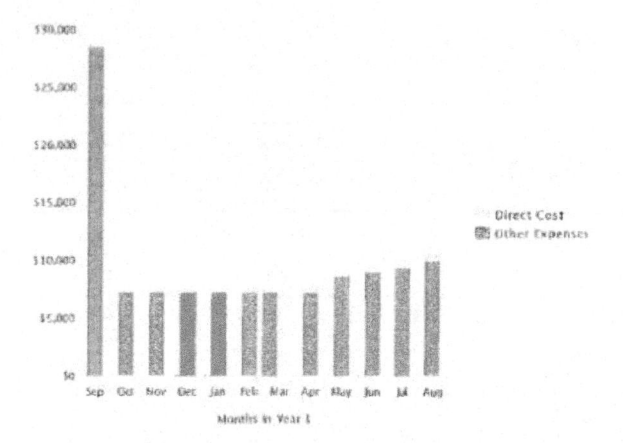

About the Budget

Marketing expenses will be higher in the first year to announce the opening of the firm and will drop after that. Most expenses will show small increases each year, as per inflationary increases and we envisage the business will remain in the same location over the first five years.

Startup Costs

Total start-up requirements would be approximately $61,000, including a starting cash in hand of $5,000. The start up costs will go into purchasing equipment required for the consultancy services as well as relevant legal costs, marketing drive, stationery and related expenses. The start-up costs are to be financed primarily by the direct owner investment.

Profit and Loss Statement

Profit and Loss Statement

	FY2016	FY2017	FY2018
Revenue	$192,000	$400,000	$550,000
Direct Cost	$3,840	$8,000	$11,000
Gross Margin	$188,160	$392,000	$539,000
Gross Margin %	98%	98%	98%
Operating Expenses			
Salary	$48,000	$86,400	$181,720
Employee Related Expenses	$4,800	$8,640	$18,172
Marketing & Promotions	$3,500	$3,000	$4,000
Rent	$3,000	$4,000	$5,000
Utilities	$1,800	$2,200	$2,800
Office Supplies	$3,600	$4,000	$4,500
Insurance	$12,000	$13,500	$15,000
Conveyance	$6,000	$7,200	$8,400
Office Maintenance	$4,595	$5,000	$5,500
Equipment Purchase	$21,200	$0	$0
Total Operating Expenses	$108,495	$133,940	$245,092
Operating Income	$79,665	$258,060	$293,908
Income Taxes	$7,967	$25,806	$29,391
Total Expenses	$120,302	$167,746	$285,483
Net Profit	$71,698	$232,254	$264,517
Net Profit / Sales	37%	58%	48%

Gross Margin by Year

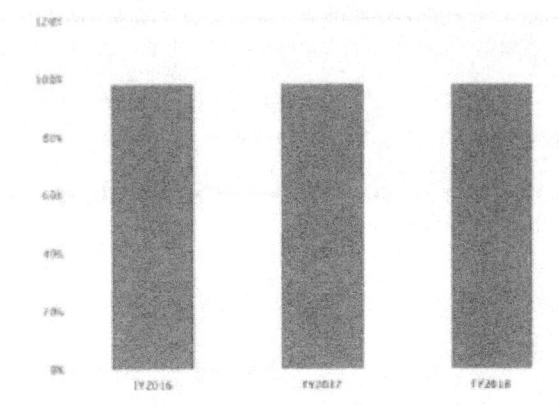

Net Profit (or Loss) by Year

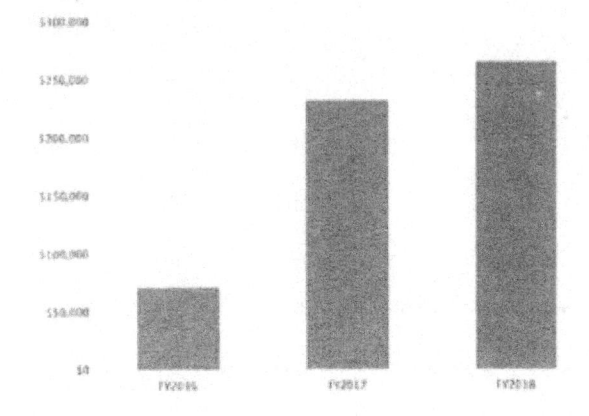

About the Profit and Loss Statement

The company generates a profit as revenue gets above the break-even line. A push on sales will be very important in generating bottom line profits.

The first year's profit will be relatively lower as we cover the initial start up costs of purchasing new equipment necessary for the consultancy services.

We do not envisage having any much interest expense but is a necessary expense on the front end of the business if we need to expand

Appendix

Revenue Forecast

Revenue Forecast Table (With Monthly Detail)

FY2016	Sep '15	Oct '15	Nov '15	Dec '15	Jan '16	Feb '16	Mar '16	Apr '16	May '16	Jun '16	Jul '16	Aug '16
Total Revenue	$5,000	$7,000	$10,000	$6,000	$7,000	$10,000	$12,000	$20,000	$25,000	$25,000	$30,000	$35,000
Total Direct Cost	$100	$140	$200	$120	$140	$200	$240	$400	$500	$520	$600	$700
Gross Margin	$4,900	$6,860	$9,800	$5,880	$6,860	$9,800	$11,760	$19,600	$24,500	$24,500	$29,400	$34,300
Gross Margin %	98%	98%	98%	98%	98%	98%	98%	98%	98%	98%	98%	98%

	FY2016	FY2017	FY2018
Total Revenue	$192,000	$400,000	$550,000
Total Direct Cost	$3,840	$8,000	$11,000
Gross Margin	$188,160	$392,000	$539,000
Gross Margin %	98%	98%	98%

Personnel Plan

Personnel Table (With Monthly Detail)

FY2016	Sep '15	Oct '15	Nov '15	Dec '15	Jan '16	Feb '16	Mar '16	Apr '16	May '16	Jun '16	Jul '15	Aug '16
Director	$4,000	$4,000	$4,000	$4,000	$4,000	$4,000	$4,000	$4,000	$4,000	$4,000	$4,000	$4,000
Operations Manager	$0	$0	$0	$0	$0	$0	$0	$0	$0	$0	$0	$0
Geotechnical Engineer	$0	$0	$0	$0	$0	$0	$0	$0	$0	$0	$0	$0
Geotechnical Technician	$0	$0	$0	$0	$0	$0	$0	$0	$0	$0	$0	$0
Engineering Technologist	$0	$0	$0	$0	$0	$0	$0	$0	$0	$0	$0	$0
CAD Drafter	$0	$0	$0	$0	$0	$0	$0	$0	$0	$0	$0	$0
Total	$4,000	$4,000	$4,000	$4,000	$4,000	$4,000	$4,000	$4,000	$4,000	$4,000	$4,000	$4,000

	FY2016	FY2017	FY2018
Director	$48,000	$56,410	$62,620
Operations Manager	$0	$34,000	$37,000
Geotechnical Engineer	$0	$0	$35,000
Geotechnical Technician	$0	$0	$20,000
Engineering Technologist	$0	$0	$28,000
CAD Drafter	$0	$0	$18,000
Total	$48,000	$86,400	$181,720

Budget

Budget Table (With Monthly Detail)

FY2016	Sep '15	Oct '15	Nov '15	Dec '15	Jan '16	Feb '16	Mar '16	Apr '16	May '16	Jun '16	Jul '16	Aug '16
Operating Expenses												
Salary	$4,000	$4,000	$4,000	$4,000	$4,000	$4,000	$4,000	$4,000	$4,000	$4,000	$4,000	$4,000
Employee Related Expenses	$400	$400	$400	$400	$400	$400	$400	$400	$400	$400	$400	$400
Marketing & Promotions	$291	$291	$291	$291	$292	$292	$292	$292	$292	$292	$292	$292
Rent	$250	$250	$250	$250	$250	$250	$250	$250	$250	$250	$250	$250
Utilities	$150	$150	$150	$150	$150	$150	$150	$150	$150	$150	$150	$150
Office Supplies	$300	$300	$300	$300	$300	$300	$300	$300	$300	$300	$300	$300
Insurance	$1,000	$1,000	$1,000	$1,000	$1,000	$1,000	$1,000	$1,000	$1,000	$1,000	$1,000	$1,000
Conveyance	$500	$500	$500	$500	$500	$500	$500	$500	$500	$500	$500	$500
Office Maintenance	$380	$380	$380	$380	$380	$380	$380	$380	$380	$380	$380	$415
Equipment Purchase	$21,200	$0	$0	$0	$0	$0	$0	$0	$0	$0	$0	$0
Total Operating Expenses	$28,471	$7,271	$7,271	$7,271	$7,272	$7,272	$7,272	$7,272	$7,272	$7,272	$7,272	$7,307

	FY2016	FY2017	FY2018
Operating Expenses			
Salary	$48,000	$86,400	$181,720
Employee Related Expenses	$4,800	$3,640	$108,592
Marketing & Promotions	$2,500	$3,300	$4,000
Rent	$3,000	$4,000	$5,000
Utilities	$1,800	$2,200	$2,800
Office Supplies	$3,600	$4,000	$4,900
Insurance	$11,000	$13,500	$16,400
Conveyance	$6,000	$7,200	$8,400
Office Maintenance	$4,385	$6,000	$8,500
Equipment Purchase	$21,200	$0	$0
Total Operating Expenses	$106,485	$133,940	$345,092

Profit and Loss Statement

Profit and Loss Statement (With Monthly Detail)

FY2016	Sep '15	Oct '15	Nov '15	Dec '15	Jan '16	Feb '16	Mar '16	Apr '16	May '16	Jun '16	Jul '16	Aug '16
Revenue	$5,000	$7,000	$10,000	$6,000	$7,000	$10,000	$12,000	$20,000	$25,000	$25,000	$30,000	$35,000
Direct Cost	$100	$140	$200	$120	$140	$200	$240	$400	$500	$500	$600	$700
Gross Margin	$4,300	$6,860	$9,800	$5,880	$6,860	$9,800	$11,760	$19,600	$24,500	$24,500	$29,400	$34,300
Gross Margin %	98%	98%	98%	98%	98%	98%	98%	98%	98%	98%	98%	98%
Operating Expenses												
Salary	$4,000	$4,000	$4,000	$4,000	$4,000	$4,000	$4,000	$4,000	$4,000	$4,000	$4,000	$4,000
Employee Related Expenses	$400	$400	$400	$400	$400	$400	$400	$400	$400	$400	$400	$400
Marketing & Promotions	$292	$292	$292	$292	$292	$292	$292	$292	$292	$292	$292	$292
Rent	$250	$250	$250	$250	$250	$250	$250	$250	$250	$250	$250	$250
Utilities	$150	$150	$150	$150	$150	$150	$150	$150	$150	$150	$150	$150
Office Supplies	$300	$300	$300	$300	$300	$300	$300	$300	$300	$300	$300	$300
Insurance	$1,000	$1,000	$1,000	$1,000	$1,000	$1,000	$1,000	$1,000	$1,000	$1,000	$1,000	$1,000
Conveyance	$500	$500	$500	$500	$500	$500	$500	$500	$500	$500	$500	$500
Office Maintenance	$380	$380	$380	$380	$380	$380	$380	$380	$380	$380	$380	$415

Equipment

Total Operating Expenses	$28,471	$7,271	$7,271	$7,271	$7,272	$7,272	$7,272	$7,272	$7,272	$7,272	$7,307
Operating Income	($23,571)	($411)	$2,329	($1,391)	($412)	$2,528	$4,488	$12,328	$17,228	$22,128	$26,993
Income Taxes	$0	$0	$0	$0	$0	$0	$0	$0	$6,122	$1,722	$2,193	$2,700
Total Expenses	$28,571	$7,411	$7,471	$7,391	$7,412	$7,472	$7,512	$7,672	$9,104	$9,494	$10,085	$10,707
Net Profit	($23,571)	($411)	$2,329	($1,391)	($412)	$2,528	$4,488	$12,328	$15,896	$15,506	$19,915	$24,293
Net Profit / Sales	(471%)	(6%)	25%	(27%)	(6%)	25%	37%	62%	64%	62%	66%	67%

	FY2016	FY2017	FY2018
Revenue	$192,000	$400,000	$550,000
Direct Cost	$3,840	$8,000	$11,000
Gross Margin	$188,160	$392,000	$539,000
Gross Margin %	98%	98%	98%
Operating Expenses			
Salary	$40,000	$84,400	$187,720
Employee Related Expenses	$4,000	$8,440	$18,772
Marketing & Promotions	$2,000	$3,000	$4,000
Rent	$3,000	$4,000	$6,000
Utilities	$1,000	$1,200	$2,000
Office Supplies	$3,600	$4,000	$4,500
Insurance	$12,000	$13,500	$15,800
Conveyance	$6,000	$7,200	$8,400
Office Maintenance	$4,395	$5,000	$5,500
Equipment Purchase	$11,200	$0	$0
Total Operating Expenses	$108,495	$133,940	$245,092
Operating Income	$79,665	$258,060	$293,908
Income Taxes	$7,967	$25,806	$29,391
Total Expenses	$120,302	$167,746	$285,483
Net Profit	$71,698	$232,254	$264,517

Section 5

Supporting Employer applicant Declaration

Page 212

"Declaration of the Applicant"

1. I, ███████, declare the following:

2. I have personal knowledge of all the facts contained in this declaration, and if called upon to testify I would do so.

3. I live at ███████████████████████████████ My children are US citizens.

4. I was born in ███████████████████████. I entered the United States in August, 1990 on an F-1 student visa. I had filed the Catholic Social Services (CSS) application in 1990. This application was prepared by Attorney, Akhter Hossain. In the CSS application, as the attached declaration will attest and I was requested to sign the application without review. The application stated that I was entered the US in 1981 when in fact that was not true.

5. Thereafter, I had filed I-687 for Status as a Temporary Resident on September 28 of 1990 to the then Immigration and Naturalization Services (INS), U.S. Department of Justice. Upon interview on the December 4, 1990, form I-688 was issued by the then INS. I had filed an application under the LIFE Act in 2000, based on CSS application.

6. I had filled out advance parole requests twice in May 1994 and December 1994, based on my CSS status. The advance parole document allowed me to briefly leave the USA (both the times less than 30 days) and they also allowed me to re-enter the USA under inspection through Los Angeles International Airport in 1994 and 1995.

7. I have completed my Bachelor of ███████████████████ from the California State University, Long Beach on August 23, 2002. I have also received a license as Professional Engineer in Civil Engineering on June 23, 2006.

8. I am an Australian citizen and I am fully qualified to apply for the treaty investor visa (E-2 visa), as Australia is a treaty country with the United States. I will fully finance the entire start-up costs and provide significant funds and employment once the E-2 would be approved.

9. I have incorporated a company in the name of " ▮▮▮▮▮▮▮▮ Works, Inc." having ▮▮ ▮▮▮. I want to invest in that company under E-2 Visa (treaty investor visitor). I am a geotechnical engineer with close to 15 years of experience in the engineering field. Currently I have been employed as a geotechnical engineer on a full time basis with Roads and Maritime Services (RMS), which is a state government organization managing the roads infrastructure for the state of New South Wales. I was employed in the private construction and engineering consultancy industry in various managerial engineering roles within NSW, Australia. Based on my work experience, in my opinion I am highly employable as a geotechnical engineer in the State of New South Wales, and other parts of the country, with potential salary of AUD$150,000.00 per year or more plus benefits.

10. I have decided to invest in this company because California is the 8th largest economy in the world and therefore, I would like to take advantage of the increased levels of construction activity that is currently being undertaken in the state. It is also expected that the opportunities will increase, as the aging infrastructure is being repaired or replaced, and new infrastructure is built for the expected increase in California population. I am also at a stage in my career where I find it more directing team engineers and marketing engineering services. My estimation indicates that at the end of the fifth year of operation, my firm is likely to make a gross of US$500,000.00 or more in annual revenue.

11. I am regretful that I overstayed in the U.S. for all the time I was there. I was there without status for more than 1 year. However, I thought I could apply for CSS and my

former attorney, Akhter Hossain prepared the CSS application and at the time just told me to sign in different places. I later learned the dates of entry and my age were not correct. I am truly sorry if that is going to be construed as fraud. However, I have a great idea for my E-2 business and I know it will be successful and I am respectfully requesting that my Waiver be granted so I can open my own company in the U.S. under the E-2 Visa.

12.

13. I regret for my mistakes and respectfully request a waiver of inadmissibility to section 212(d)(3) of the INA, so that I may be temporarily admitted into the United States as an investor visitor on a E-2 visa.

Declarant:

Made in the USA
Las Vegas, NV
28 January 2024